VICTORY

FAVORS THE

FEARLESS

By Darrin Donnelly

THINK LIKE A WARRIOR
The Five Inner Beliefs That Make You Unstoppable

OLD SCHOOL GRIT
Times May Change, But the Rules for Success Never Do

RELENTLESS OPTIMISM
How a Commitment to Positive Thinking Changes Everything

LIFE TO THE FULLEST
A Story About Finding Your Purpose and Following Your Heart

VICTORY FAVORS THE FEARLESS
How to Defeat the 7 Fears That Hold You Back

VICTORY

FAVORS THE

FEARLESS

HOW TO
DEFEAT THE 7 FEARS
THAT HOLD YOU BACK

Darrin Donnelly

Sports for the Soul

Stories of Faith, Family, Courage, and Character.

This book is part of the *Sports for the Soul* series. For updates on this book, a sneak peek at future books, and a free newsletter that delivers advice and inspiration from top coaches, athletes, and sports psychologists, join us at: **SportsForTheSoul.com**.

The *Sports for the Soul* newsletter will help you:

- Find your calling and follow your passion
- Harness the power of positive thinking
- Build your self-confidence
- Attack every day with joy and enthusiasm
- Develop mental toughness
- Increase your energy and stay motivated
- Explore the spiritual side of success
- Be a positive leader for your family and your team
- Become the best version of yourself
- And much more…

Join us at: **SportsForTheSoul.com**.

To Laura, Patrick, Katie, and Tommy;
who are everything to me.

Contents

Introduction

You become what you think about most.

Neuroscientists tell us that our brains are rewired based on the intensity and repetition of the thoughts we think. This is not a metaphor. The neural pathways in your brain are actually rewired by the consistent thoughts you think. The more often and the more intensely you think about something, the more proficiently those positive or negative thoughts drive every subsequent thought you think, decision you make, and action you take. If you think negative thoughts over and over again, your mental outlook will quite literally get "stuck in a rut."

Everything you do follows your mental outlook. That is how "you become what you think about," as psychologists say. And that is why it's so important to protect your mindset and proactively take control of your thoughts.

Fearful thinking is one of the most damaging and

destructive thought patterns you can fall into.

Fears are usually *repetitive* — you tend to ruminate about them over and over again. Fears are also *intense* — they can weigh you down and make it hard to think about anything else. This combination of frequency and intensity is why fear is such a damaging emotion.

Your fears hold you back from living the life you were born to live. If you're ever going to achieve success, happiness, and peace of mind, you must first defeat your fears.

Fear is the strong, unpleasant emotion that *expects* something bad to happen. It is the root cause of every negative thought that eats away at your self-confidence and every worry that keeps you up at night.

Fear is the voice that makes you doubt yourself. It is the voice that tells you to quit, that you shouldn't bother trying, and that you don't have what it takes to be successful.

Being in a state of fear makes you tight, timid, and indecisive. It makes you worry incessantly about all the things that *could* go wrong in the future.

Whenever you find yourself worrying, stressing,

procrastinating, or questioning your potential — fear is getting the best of you.

The good news is that fear *can* be defeated. You can win the inner battle against fear and this book will show you how to do it.

Specifically, there are seven common fears you must learn to defeat if you want to live a happy and successful life:

1) The fear of what other people think.

2) The fear of change.

3) The fear of making the wrong decision.

4) The fear of missing out on something better.

5) The fear of not being good enough.

6) The fear of failure being permanent.

7) The fear of being "due" for a setback.

In some form or another, every major worry and self-destructive thought is rooted in one of these seven fears.

Like previous books in the *Sports for the Soul* series, this book is an inspirational fable set in the world of sports. It's the story of a boxer, Mickey McGavin, who must learn to defeat the seven fears that are holding him back — in the ring and in life.

Each time he learns to defeat one of these

debilitating fears, it propels him closer to his ultimate goal: a shot at the heavyweight championship of the world. Mickey learns from a wise trainer that he must first defeat the fear in his mind if he's going to have any chance of defeating his opponent in the ring.

This is a story about what happens when a man unleashes his true potential by overcoming his fears. It's a story about how to become *fearless* in the face of adversity.

Boxing is the metaphor for life in this story, but the techniques used for defeating fear are universal. No matter your profession, fear is your ultimate opponent. The boxer who fears losing his next fight must contend with the exact same fears the salesperson has about the next sale, the speaker has about the next speech, the entrepreneur has about the next product launch, or you may have about taking the risk and going after your biggest dreams.

To defeat fear, you must have a fighter's mentality. You must attack fear head-on. That's the only way to beat it.

I believe there is an inner power locked inside every person and the only way to unleash it is to develop a fearless attitude that dreams big and attacks life.

The thoughts we choose to think make us who we are. This book will show you why it's so important to conquer your fears and why victory—in sports, in business, and in life—always favors the fearless.

There's no reason to let fear hold you back any longer. You can *choose* to be fearless. You can *choose* to be victorious in the game of life.

Darrin Donnelly
SportsForTheSoul.com

"He who is not courageous enough to take risks will accomplish nothing in life."

- MUHAMMAD ALI

★★★ 1 ★★★
PREFIGHT

Patterson vs. McGavin
MOMENTS BEFORE THE FIGHT…

I hear the sound of the crowd rumbling through the cement walls that surround me in the locker room. The undercard fights are over. The anticipation is rising for the main event.

I'm sitting on a high table, my eyes downward, watching as the official assigned by the state athletic commission takes out a black marker and initials the white tape on my fists, indicating that he has okayed the tape-job he just watched Terry, one of my cornermen, complete.

Andre, my manager and trainer, picks up one of my boxing gloves and holds it open as I slip my right hand inside for a tight fit. Then the left. As each hand slips snugly into the glove, I feel *power* — like an ignition switch has just been flipped on.

Terry quickly ties the glove strings around my wrists, then runs tape around them. The state official again scribbles his initials over the tape.

Both gloves are secure. I'm locked in.

"Good luck to you," the official says to me with a nod.

"Thanks," I say, my voice higher and quieter than I expect.

He exits our locker room and I bang my gloves together twice. I move my head quickly from one side to the other and I hear two quick pops in my neck as it loosens up. I slide off the table. As my feet hit the floor, I inhale deeply and exhale slowly.

This is it. It's go time.

My name is Mickey McGavin. Eight years ago, I was a faceless Kansas City bartender dreaming of becoming a world-class boxer. Tonight, I'm fighting for the heavyweight championship of the world in a match that will be seen by millions of boxing fans.

Everything I've been through — all the sacrifices I've made, all the ups and downs, all the struggles and frustrations, all the lessons learned — has led me to this moment. The opportunity of a lifetime.

And yet, I'd rather be almost anywhere else in the world than where I am right now.

That's the fear talking.

I'm about to face the most dangerous man on the planet: Bruno Patterson. To fight fans, he's known as "The British Bomber" and it's a nickname that suits him well. He is the undefeated, undisputed heavyweight champion of the world. He is 6-foot-6, 265 pounds, and his combination of size, power, and hand speed has captivated the sports world and revived boxing's heavyweight division. While most fighters his size tend to rely on long jabs and an advantageous reach to wear down smaller opponents, Patterson is a knockout artist who uses brute force to dispose of his opponents quickly. In a few moments, he will try to do the same to me.

I've seen the damage he can do. Like everyone else, I've watched his devastating knockouts again and again. Twice, I've seen him knock top-ranked fighters out cold. Just eight months ago, he faced the world's No. 1-ranked heavyweight contender, Terrance "T.N.T" Thompson, and Patterson knocked him out in the third round. The weary contender suffered a broken jaw and had to be carried out on a stretcher.

Two years ago, I fought Thompson myself and *I* was the the one who got knocked out. This is yet another reason why I'm a huge underdog in tonight's fight.

Standing in the locker room, I replay Patterson's brutal knockouts in my head. Over and over, I see him landing power shots that opponents don't wake up from. In my head, the opponent Patterson is knocking out starts to look a lot like...*me*. I see his fist slamming into my jaw. I see my face hitting the canvas. I see myself limping back to the locker room, my head tucked in shame.

That's fear trying to take control of my mind.

Fear says to run. Fear says you don't deserve to be in the same ring with Patterson. Fear says you're going to get hurt. Fear says you're going to embarrass yourself in front of the world.

Fear reminds me that I'm nothing more than a "tune-up" fight for the champ. He wants a quick win and an easy paycheck before his next *real* fight against the sport's latest No. 1 contender. I'm ranked No. 6 and, with a record of 33-5-1, do I even deserve to be ranked that high?

Fear reminds me that I'm a 12-to-1 underdog. I'm

only here because I got "lucky" in my last two fights and because the No. 1 contender — the fighter who "deserves" this match — wanted more time to prepare for his title shot. It's been reported that two young, up-and-coming contenders turned down this fight. They have futures to worry about. I don't. I'm 31 years old and running out of time. This is my lone shot at achieving something truly great in this sport. Lose tonight and I'll never again get an opportunity like this. I probably never should have gotten this opportunity in the first place. *You don't belong in this ring,* fear says.

But fear is a liar.

I'm all too familiar with these feelings right before a fight. Fear gets loudest at these moments. I've heard fear screaming at me like this before every fight I've ever been in, regardless of who my opponent was — the ranked contenders with impeccable records *and* the journeyman fighters with losing records. I felt this fear before my amateur fights as a kid. I felt this fear before football games back in high school and college. I've heard fear's lies before taking tests, before job interviews, before my wedding day, before anything of importance.

Different degrees of fear for different events, but fear nonetheless. Fear tells me I'm not good enough, that I don't deserve something this important to me.

The fear is far more intense tonight. The physical danger I'm about to face has heightened the fear to a nearly unbearable level.

"Fear is simply confirmation that what you're about to do is very important to you," Andre told me years ago. "Recognizing your fear isn't admitting weakness; it's admitting reality. You can't defeat an opponent by pretending it doesn't exist. And fear is the biggest, baddest opponent you'll ever face."

I wouldn't be here if it wasn't for Andre. He's the former world champion who saved my career and turned me into the fighter — and the man — that I am today.

Andre has always reminded me: the bigger the moment, the bigger the fear.

Tonight, the fear is bigger than it's ever been before. I have to defeat it. It's starting to overwhelm me. My heart is beating loud and fast, my hands are shaking slightly, sweat gathers on my forehead.

I wish I could close my eyes and travel an hour-and-a-half into the future. I wish I could wake up *after* the fight. How did I do? Win or lose, at least it would be over.

That's the fear talking. It won't shut up.

"You'll never defeat the opponent in the ring until you first defeat the fear in you," Andre has told me many times over the last eight years. I can't let fear win.

I force myself to replace the image of getting knocked out by Patterson with new visions: me landing the knockout punch and sending the champ to the canvas, me withstanding his biggest blows and holding my ground, me lifting the championship belt high above my head after tonight's match, and me embracing Rachel after the fight with the belt flung over my shoulder, just like Rocky and Adrian in the movies.

I remind myself that the anticipation is always worse than the actual fight. It's the moment before an event when fear is the loudest. Once the event starts, all I can do is act. And *action conquers fear*.

It's time to take action.

Andre's hands are now covered by leather punching mitts. He holds them up in front of me. My targets. I unleash several combinations. Pop-pop-pop.

Side-to-side, side-to-side. Pop-pop, pop-pop. It's a training sequence I've been through thousands of times. I don't have to think. I let go. I snap crisp, powerful punches at the mitts.

The fear dissipates just a little bit more with each punch.

Action conquers fear.

That's another message Andre has repeated often through the years. The man knows more about fighting — in the ring and out — than anyone I know.

And he's right. With each punch, the fear gets pushed out of my mind.

A few more combinations, with the power behind my punches intensifying each time. Then Andre throws off the mitts. He steps in front of me and looks me in the eye.

"You're ready for this," he says. "You weren't ready four years ago. You weren't ready one year ago. You weren't ready last week. But you are ready *now*. Everything you've been through, everything that has happened to you, it all happened *for* you, bringing you to this moment. There are no accidents. You're here — right now — because you were born to be here. You're here because you deserve it. God doesn't make mistakes. You wouldn't have this opportunity if you weren't ready for it. There's nowhere else in the world you're supposed to be right now than right here in this very moment. You belong here."

I nod, feeling adrenaline rush through my veins, blasting away the fear that's been trying to thicken up my blood.

Terry helps me put my robe on as Andre says, "Believe me with your whole heart when I tell you: *you are ready*. This is your moment. You've built yourself into a champion. That champion is inside you…waiting. It's time to unleash it."

I nod again and punch my gloves together. I take another deep breath, releasing more fear. Gotta get it out of my system. Throwing punches helps. Deep breathing helps. Empowering self-talk helps.

I'm strong, I'm healthy, I'm blessed, I say to myself. *With God by my side, I can accomplish anything.*

With every inhale, I envision pure power filling up my body. With every exhale, I envision fear leaving and evaporating in the air. This visualization technique is one of the first things Andre taught me back when he started training me.

"Let's go," Andre says.

He turns and leads the way as he pushes open the heavy locker-room door.

The crowd noise is louder in the hallway outside the locker room. A guy in a suit holding a walkie talkie says to us, "Ready?"

Andre nods. The guy in the suit says something into his walkie talkie and then holds it up to his ear. He nods, looks to us, and says, "Follow me."

We follow him down the hallway and stop in front of a black curtain. Behind that curtain, my destiny awaits. Fear rises again, not as powerful as it was just moments ago. Still, it's there, this time in my stomach. I bounce on my toes, trying to stay loose, trying to stay active. I take a deep breath and try to exhale the fear.

The lights go out in the arena behind the curtain. The crowd lets out a deafening roar.

I hear the opening chords of my entrance music: "I'm Shipping Up to Boston" by the Dropkick Murphys. I'm not from Boston and I'm not even sure what the song is about, but the Celtic beat and loud guitars always get me jacked up. The crowd loves it too. The curtain opens and the crowd roars even louder.

As I begin my walk down the aisle, a spotlight

shines on me and the house lights slowly come back on, illuminating the sold-out arena.

I don't make eye contact with anyone, but I can *feel* the crowd that surrounds me jumping to the beat of the song as I make my way up the aisle. I focus my eyes on one thing and one thing only: the ring. It sits there, under the lights, waiting for me.

This is the gladiator walk. That moment before the biggest battle of my life.

Once I'm in the ring, I block everything out. I bounce lightly, staying loose, moving side-to-side.

Then, the house lights go out and a new song begins. My opponent, the heavyweight champion of the world, makes his way to the ring amidst entrance music of his own and pyrotechnic explosions along the way. I couldn't tell you what the song was or exactly what type of pyro effects shot off around him. It's all a blur to me. I've got my eyes directed at the canvas floor as I throw light punches into the air.

I can't allow myself to be distracted.

I can't allow myself to be intimidated.

When Bruno Patterson finally enters the ring, I immediately notice his size. He looks bigger and stronger than he did at yesterday's weigh-in. I notice his height and wonder how I can possibly go toe-to-toe with a guy this tall. His massive traps, shoulders, and biceps represent the shear force that is about to destroy me. Patterson is suddenly much more imposing than he was just 24 hours ago.

You don't stand a chance with this guy, the voice of fear says. Fear makes its physical presence known in my stomach once again.

I make eye contact with Patterson. He gives me an icy stare and fear gets louder: *He's a killer and you're his prey.*

That's exactly what Patterson—and every other fighter I've faced—wants me to feel.

The first step in defeating fear is recognizing its voice. That's another lesson Andre taught me. Recognize it, block it, then battle it back. Don't passively allow fear to have its way with you.

I counter fear with a message of my own: *This is my night. I am unstoppable. I am a champion.*

"This is your night," Andre says behind me—almost as though he can read my thoughts. "You're ready. Tonight, you're the greatest fighter in the world. Embrace who you are. Unleash the champion inside."

I trust Andre. His words carry more weight than the voice of fear inside me. When he tells me to embrace the champion that I am, I feel my chest puff out and my chin lift higher. I stare at Patterson and portray…confidence.

Bring it on, Bruno. I'm ready for you.

Patterson flashes a confident smirk, breaks our stare-down, and turns to wave at the crowd.

The announcer does his thing, but I don't hear a word of it. I tune everything out.

Patterson and I meet in the center of the ring, the referee gives final instructions, and we touch gloves without saying a word.

Back to my corner one last time before the fight. Facing my corner, I bow my head and say a quick prayer. After I make the Sign of the Cross, Andre grabs my shoulders, looks me straight in the eyes, and says, "Unleash it."

He doesn't tell me to "prove it." He doesn't tell me to "earn it." He tells me to "unleash it."

It's his way of saying, you already have the power, you've already put in the work and preparation. You don't have to prove anything. You simply have to unleash the champion that you are.

I nod, then turn around to face Patterson across the ring in his corner. I feel at least a foot taller than I did just moments ago. One last exhale followed by a big inhale.

Exhaling the fear, inhaling the power.

All the energy in this arena is focused on us and I'm going to harness it.

The bell rings.

The crowd cheers.

Patterson and I converge in the center of the ring and the combat begins.

★★★ 2 ★★★
FIRED

EIGHT YEARS EARLIER...

If someone had told my 23-year-old self that I'd be fighting for the heavyweight championship of the world in eight years, I would have never believed it. I would not have believed it because my 23-year-old self thought his boxing career was over after just six fights.

"I think it's time for you to retire," my first trainer, Marco, said to me two days after the sixth fight of my professional career.

Marco was considered the top trainer in Kansas City and when I risked everything to chase my dream of becoming a pro boxer, I begged him to train me. He told me he didn't train heavyweights, but if I could lose 35 pounds and drop down to cruiserweight (a weight class with a 200-pound limit), he'd consider it.

Six months later, I showed up at his gym weighing 198. He trained me—reluctantly—for the next 18 months.

Marco called me into his office the Monday after my third loss—a fight I lost by technical knockout after Marco threw in the towel late in the third round. The loss dropped my record to two wins, three losses, and one draw.

As I sat in his office, I had stitches over my black-and-blue right eye and the left side of my face was swelled up to the point that it looked like I had stuffed my cheek with marbles.

"Look at yourself," he said, leaning back in his creaky metal chair behind his messy desk. "This sport ain't for you."

"Thanks for the vote of confidence," I said.

"It's time to move on," Marco said, now fumbling through papers on his desk as though he'd lost interest in me.

"What are you talking about?" I said, realizing this wasn't some type of motivational ploy. "Move on to what?"

"A new career."

"You're firing me?"

"It's for your own good," he said. "Look, kid, I train contenders. I've seen what happens to fighters like you."

"Fighters like me?"

Marco looked up at me. "Yeah, fighters like you. Guys who start boxing because they think it'll prove their manhood or something. Guys who should've never stepped into the ring in the first place and now they don't know when to quit. I've seen it before. Guys like you don't end up so good and I don't want any part of it. I train contenders."

"How do you know if I'm a contender? I'm just getting started."

"Two years, six fights, you've never had a winning record. I've seen enough. I gave you a shot, Mickey. It's time to move on."

Marco said it so matter-of-factly, barely making eye contact with me as he turned his attention back to the jumbled stacks of paper on his desk. He either didn't know or didn't care that he was stomping on the dream I'd carried with me since I was nine years old.

"Just like that, you're quitting on me?" I said.

Marco shrugged as he looked back up at me. "Whaddaya want from me? We tried, it didn't work out. Not everyone is born to be a champion. You got plenty of things you can do with your life. Go back to college, finish your degree. Half the guys I train don't have high school degrees. They *need* this world, you don't. You got options, they don't. I'm doing this for your own good. You'll thank me someday."

I had heard it all before. People thought I was crazy for leaving college to chase my dream of becoming a professional boxer. I had spent three years playing football on a half-scholarship at a Division II college when I decided it was now-or-never if I wanted to become a fighter. From the outside, I understood how it must have looked: a rarely-used fullback at a small college who saw one too many *Rocky* movies and suddenly decided he was going to become a pro boxer.

But that's not how it happened.

I started boxing when I was nine, less than a year after my mother left our family and never came back.

When she left, Dad was blindsided. His life was turned upside down. A traditional, old-school kind of guy, Dad never imagined he'd be a single father raising four boys on his own. But, that's exactly where he found himself in his forties, catching naps between jobs while he tried to provide for his sons.

My dad was a cop and he worked long hours. He was always trying to get overtime to make ends meet and when he wasn't working as a cop, he was doing odd jobs like building decks, hanging drywall, and picking up bartending shifts at Gerry's Pub—a legacy that I would later continue.

Whenever I did see my dad, he was kind, but quiet—always distant and stewing about something. He worked hard to provide for us—that I knew—but I never really got to know him.

Less than a year after my mom left, Dad got fed up when two of my older brothers nearly got kicked out of school for a prank they pulled. Dad wasn't going to put up with that. He signed all four of us up at a place called Bruno's Gym. It was a local boxing gym started by two cops decades ago as a way to keep kids out of trouble. Dad had been recommending the gym to kids he met on the streets for years. I guess he figured if it was a good enough way to keep those kids out of trouble, it would be good enough for his own kids.

We were told to be there every day after school. Dad's intention may have been to simply keep us busy and out of trouble, but the sport of boxing changed my life. My older brothers liked the sport okay, but going to the gym every day felt like something they *had* to do, not something they wanted to do.

I, on the other hand, fell in love with boxing. The gym became my second home. I couldn't wait to get there each day after school. It was the place where I felt safest—the place where the world made sense to me. It was a place where I felt like I fit in.

Dad somehow managed to send us to Catholic school (he knew he wouldn't be around enough to teach us the importance of faith himself). Coming from a single-parent household was uncommon at my school and I was jealous of all the kids who had smiling moms and dads picking them up from school and organizing get-togethers with other kids. I hated hearing about all the fun weekend activities everyone else got to participate in with their families. I was self-conscious about the hand-me-down clothes I wore. I was small for my age and struggled in most sports. I would hear about parties that everyone except me got invited to. In those early grade-school days, I was insecure and felt like a loner—like I didn't really belong.

But at Bruno's Gym, all the kids were from single-parent homes and each of us rarely saw the parent we did live with. I didn't feel like an outcast at Bruno's. In fact, the gym made me feel lucky because I saw kids who had it worse than me. At least I had my brothers. At least I had a father who loved me—even if I didn't see him much.

And though I was small for my age, I took to boxing much better than other sports. (It helped that boxing grouped you by weight class, so I was able to compete against kids my size.) I loved being at the gym. I loved the action of boxing, the sweat, the blood, the contact, the competition, the soreness after a grueling workout, and the camaraderie with the other fighters. I loved the feeling of pushing myself further each day—walking out of the gym and being able to say to myself, *Today, I got better.*

I also loved how in boxing nobody could deny you what you earned. It didn't matter who you were or where you came from; if you worked hard, you got results. It was the one area of my life where I felt like I was in control. If I worked hard enough, there was nothing and nobody that could stop me.

As I grew up, boxing became my life's passion and I dreamed of becoming a champion. I competed in a few amateur tournaments, winning one and finishing third in two others.

Halfway through high school, I *finally* hit a growth spurt and quickly surpassed a lot of the guys my age. Everyone urged me to focus on football. Though I loved boxing, they said football was a much more "practical" sport to play and that I might be able to earn a scholarship if I focused on it. They were right. I earned a half-scholarship to a small local college. Though I still found myself daydreaming about one day returning to boxing, football was my focus.

In the winter of my junior year at college, one of my brothers called to tell me Dad had suffered a massive heart attack. By the time I made it to the hospital, Dad had passed away. He was 55 years old and had died just one week after retiring from the police force.

That moment changed everything for me.

I realized that tomorrow was promised to no one.

All his life, Dad looked forward to retirement — it was that "someday" when he would be able to spend more time with his sons, he told us. But that someday never came. He was gone before he could experience it.

I spent the spring semester pondering my future

and questioning what I was doing with my life. *What are my dreams? Life is short, am I living it the way I should be? What would I be if I could be anything?*

These questions kept bringing me back to the sport I had fallen in love with when I was nine years old.

If boxing is what you want to do with your life, why aren't you doing it? I asked myself. *Time moves fast and you're not getting any younger. What are you waiting for? Nobody's going to hand you your dreams. If you want it, you have to go out and get it.*

I couldn't ignore my passion any longer. I told my position coach I was leaving college to pursue a boxing career and he laughed me out of the room. He told me I was making the biggest mistake of my life. He was the first of many to express such a sentiment.

The only people who supported this dream of mine were my three older brothers and Rachel, my high school sweetheart and the woman I married just three months before Marco gave me the boot. Rachel knew how passionate I was about boxing. She knew how much this dream meant to me.

But when I told Rachel about Marco firing me, she wasn't exactly heartbroken.

"Maybe he's right," she said after initially trying to

console me. "Now that we're married, maybe it's time for you to go back to school, start teaching, and then we can start a family."

Up to this point, after paying Marco management and training fees, I hadn't made a dime as a fighter. In fact, I was *losing* money chasing this dream. I was a bartender at night—mainly because it freed up my days to train, but also because it paid me just enough to cover meals and training.

Rachel had graduated from college and started an entry-level office job. We were sitting on maxed-out credit cards, zero savings, and tens of thousands of dollars in student-loan debt. The hole we were digging was getting deeper each month and I wasn't contributing anything to stop the bleeding.

I could understand Rachel's reaction. From a financial perspective, me retiring from boxing made perfect sense. It would be the *responsible* thing for me to do.

Plus, this *was* part of the deal. I had promised Rachel (and myself) that if fighting didn't work out, I'd go back to school. But I didn't expect my boxing career to end so quickly. Just six professional fights? One of my three losses was a six-round draw that could have easily gone my way. One was a split-decision after four rounds — another one that could have gone my way. Give me those two fights and I'm 4-2, a much more respectable start to my career.

It wasn't supposed to end this way — not this fast, not with a losing record, and not with such an embarrassing final match (I had been bloodied and knocked down three times before Marco threw in the towel to end the fight).

In the days after Marco fired me, I began to accept the fact that my dream of making it as a pro boxer was over. It was time to move on. Just like so many people had told me, it was a silly idea from the start. It was time to grow up and be a husband who could contribute to his family.

I started looking into the application process at some local colleges while asking for more shifts at Gerry's Pub, the bar I worked at.

Everyone was right about me. I didn't belong in a boxing ring. I had wasted the last two years of my life and I was making a fool of myself trying to prove I could be a successful fighter.

Who am I kidding? I'm embarrassing myself thinking I could make it in boxing.

Just like that, the dream was over. Over before it ever began. I tried and failed miserably. That was that.

Or so I thought.

I would learn later that every setback is a setup for something greater. Though I didn't know it at the time, getting fired by Marco ended up being one of the best things that ever happened to me.

★★★ 3 ★★★
EVERYTHING IS A CHOICE

I was working behind the bar and feeling sorry for myself on a quiet weeknight at Gerry's Pub when Andre Holiday walked in. I recognized him right away.

The former super middleweight champion of the world was a legend in Kansas City. A local hero who rose to the very top of his profession and inspired the sports world with his courageous story. I was only two years old when he won his title in 1989, but he was a hero to me just like he was to everyone else in this city.

He walked into the bar with his chest high and his broad shoulders pushed back. He looked like he would probably fight as a heavyweight these days, but as a strong and trim heavyweight. He was sharply dressed and had a pronounced bounce in his step. He exuded confidence, but also flashed an approachable smile.

As he walked into the bar, he nodded at the first person he saw — a patron who did a quick double-take before asking if he could shake Andre's hand and take a picture with him. "Of course," Andre said with a smile. As the patron snapped the selfie, Andre held his fist up to the guy's chin — a pose every former champion seems to have perfected.

If it hadn't been for the gray stubble in his beard, I would have thought Andre was still a pro athlete.

After taking a picture and signing an autograph for the guy who first noticed him, Andre walked up to the bar and I extended my hand. "Welcome to Gerry's, champ."

He shook my hand. A very firm handshake, one of the firmest I've ever shaken. The guy still had dynamite in his fists.

"What can I get you?" I asked.

"Just a water," he said. "I'm here on business."

"Yeah? Looking for someone?"

"I've already found him. I'm here to see you."

The surprised look on my face made him laugh.

"You're Mickey McGavin, aren't you?"

"I am," I said, wondering why this former world

champion was looking for me.

"Well, I hear you're retiring from the fight game, but you look too young to retire."

"It's not by choice," I said with an uncomfortable chuckle.

"**Everything is a choice**," Andre shot back. "**And the choices you make, make you.**"

"My trainer gave me the boot," I said. "It wasn't my decision."

"But you haven't been looking for another trainer, have you?"

I lowered my eyes. "Uh...I guess not." I had reasoned that if the best trainer in the city didn't want anything to do with me, why would any other trainer?

"So, there you go," Andre said. "You made the *choice* to accept your trainer's opinion that you should retire. **I believe there are two types of people in this world: Those who believe success is a choice and those who make excuses for why they're not successful.**"

I shot Andre a defensive glare. "You trying to kick a man when he's down?" As I said that, the stitches above my still-bruised right eye gave me an itch, reminding me how I must have looked at the moment.

"Not at all," Andre said with a smile. "I came here to tell you I think it's a mistake."

"What's a mistake?"

"You retiring," Andre said. "I've watched you fight. I think you've got something. It's raw and it only seems to come out when you're not overcome with fear, but it's there. I think you've got something special and it would be a mistake to walk away."

I took a moment to wrap my head around what was happening. One of the city's most beloved heroes, a former world champion and a man I had never met before, just walked into the bar looking for *me*, a beat-up fighter that the sport had quickly chewed up and spit out. And this champion wanted to talk me out of quitting. Where was this coming from?

"I think you're the first person to tell me it would be a *mistake* for me to stop fighting," I said.

"I don't doubt that," Andre said. "And I believe it's that type of thinking that is keeping you from becoming the fighter you could become. You just need to find the right man to guide you. You need to find someone who can help you overcome all that fear holding you back."

"What are you proposing?"

Andre smiled big. "Mickey, I'd like to be your trainer."

It's hard to put into words just how surreal this moment was. Here I was, at one of the lowest points in my life—coming to terms with the fact that my dream of pro boxing was over because nobody wanted anything to do with me—and in walks a former world champ to not only tell me I should keep fighting, but also that he wants to train me.

You have to understand who Andre Holiday was and what he meant to this city. He climbed the boxing ranks back in the 1980s—a time when boxing's middleweight division was the best it had ever been with fighters like Sugar Ray Leonard, "Marvelous" Marvin Hagler, Thomas "The Hitman" Hearns, and Roberto Duran dominating the sport.

Andre became a popular fighter because of his perseverance. He lost four times in his career, but avenged each one of those losses. In 47 professional fights, he was knocked down *sixteen* times...but never knocked out. He had an almost miraculous ability to get back up from the canvas and take back the fight.

In 1989, at the age of 29, it was finally Andre's turn

to stand atop his crowded division and he became the undisputed super middleweight champion of the world.

But that's not what Andre Holiday is best known for. What he's best known for is what happened *after* he won the title.

A week after winning the belt, Andre bought himself a new car to celebrate the victory. On a rainy summer night, he lost control of that car and crashed it into a telephone pole.

He survived the gruesome wreck, but spent weeks in the hospital. He broke multiple bones and smashed up his left hip and shoulder. Despite several surgeries and months of intense rehab, Andre's shoulder and hip never fully recovered. He couldn't snap punches the way he once did and to this day he walked with an uneven gait — though Andre had turned his would-be limp into a confident bounce.

An instant after reaching the top of his profession and seeing his years of hard work pay off with a world championship, his career was over. It was a story that could have been just another unlucky tragedy in the sports history books.

But that's not where this story ends.

What made Andre Holiday one of the most beloved sports figures in this city's history was how he responded to his career-ending car wreck.

When it was clear he could no longer participate in the sport he loved so dearly, Andre reexamined his life and his faith. He went to college, earned a degree in Psychology, and got heavily involved with his church. Soon, he was showing up on TV delivering inspirational messages about how everything happens for a reason. He became a sought-after motivational speaker, then a bestselling author, then a serial entrepreneur, and then a real estate developer. Wherever he went, he preached a message of faith, hope, and optimism. His enthusiasm was contagious. He endeared himself even more to the city with his unending charitable work and fundraising efforts. He was always lending a hand, always helping raise money for various causes.

Everyone loved the champ. For his feats in the ring, yes, but also for being the walking embodiment of optimism and perseverance. He believed anything was possible and whenever you read his books or heard him speak, you came away believing the same thing.

And now, here he was, talking to me as I served drinks at Gerry's Pub and trying to convince me not to quit on my dream.

Feeling as though this was all just a little too good to be true, I asked Andre, "Why me?"

"I told you, because I see something special in you," Andre said.

"My old manager just fired me because he was certain there *isn't* anything special in me."

"I know," Andre said, "and I was ecstatic to hear that Marco has such poor judgment. You see, I've been scouting local fighters for awhile now and you caught my attention several months ago. But, since you already had a trainer, I didn't want to step on anybody's toes.

"Are you a religious man, Mickey?"

That caught me off guard. I shrugged and responded awkwardly. "Sort of. I pray, I believe. I need to get better about it."

"Well, I believe too. And when I hear God calling, I listen. For a long time, I've felt called back to boxing.

I just turned 50 a few weeks ago and it hit me that I'm not getting any younger. It's time to start the next chapter of my life and that chapter is my return to the sport I love — the sport that taught me so much about life.

"I've been looking for someone I feel called to train. When I watch you fight, Mickey, I see something special buried underneath all that fear and I want to help you unleash it. When I heard Marco dropped you, I knew God was intervening, telling me *you* were the one — the one I needed to train. I don't know how I know, I just do."

"You keep mentioning fear," I said. "You think I fight scared?"

Andre nodded. "I do. But I can help you conquer your fear. And once you learn how to knock out your fear, you can start knocking out your opponents."

I liked the sound of that.

"Life is all about the choices you make," Andre said. "I'm offering you a choice right now. I'm a trainer who has never trained anybody before and you're a fighter who has never had a winning record. What do you say we give each other a shot?"

Andre stuck out his hand for me to shake.

When you find yourself fired by your previous trainer and a former world champion shows up out of the blue, extends his hand, and offers to train you, you *don't* turn him down.

"How can I possibly say no?" I said.

I shook his hand and felt electricity. I knew my life was about to change.

★★★ 4 ★★★
THE FIGHT AGAINST FEAR

The first lesson Andre taught me not only changed the way I saw myself as a fighter, it changed the way I saw the world.

"I went through the film of all your fights last night and I'm surprised you won any of them," Andre said.

I turned my head away from the heavy bag I was punching. "Gee thanks, Coach."

This was my first week of training with Andre. He had a large country estate outside of the city. On his property was a big barn, which he converted into his own personal boxing gym. That gym became my new training facility.

"I'm serious," Andre said. "If it hadn't been for the couple times you stopped thinking and unleashed your power, you never would have won a fight."

I wasn't sure if that was supposed to be a compliment or an insult, but I continued to work the heavy bag as I listened.

"You barely ever show your power," Andre continued. "You're always dancing. And wincing. Dancing and wincing. I can see the wheels turning when you fight. You think too much. You're too tight. You fight scared."

At that, I threw one big power shot to the heavy bag, then dropped my hands and turned to Andre. "Is this supposed to motivate me or something? If it is, it isn't working."

"I'm just telling you what I saw. You fight scared. You let fear dictate the fight. I'm wondering why you do that. What are you afraid of when you're in that ring?"

I shrugged, annoyed. "I don't know what you want me to say."

"There were a few times where you stopped thinking during your fights. You loosened up, let go of the fear, and started fighting. That's when you looked special. Raw, but special. Unfortunately, those were rare moments. I want you to tell me what you're afraid of."

"Marco taught me that it was good to be afraid in the ring. He told me fear is a weapon. He said fear is a good thing because it motivates you, it makes you try harder, it makes you respect your opponent."

Andre handed me a water bottle. This was his way of telling me it was time to take a break and listen to him. It was time to pause the physical training and focus on the mental training.

"A lot of trainers think that way," Andre said. "Marco is right that fear can be used as a powerful weapon. Mike Tyson famously said he used fear as a weapon, but he used fear as a weapon *against* his opponents. He intimidated his opponent so much before the fight that it was over before it began. Tyson believed that if he could fill his opponent with fear, he could easily win the fight. And he was right. But notice that his opponents were the ones full of fear. Fear was a weapon only if he could force his opponent to be more scared than he was. Think about that the next time somebody tells you fear is good for you. If fear is *good* for you, why did champions like Tyson want their opponents to be full of it?"

"I guess I didn't think about it that way," I said before taking a swig of water.

"Tyson knew that if his opponent was full of fear, that opponent would be timid. He would be tight and anxious. He would be indecisive and he would make more mistakes. That made him an easy target."

"But being afraid of your opponent makes you try harder," I said. "If I don't fear my opponent, I won't be as motivated to work hard preparing for him. That would be reckless of me. I won't protect myself if I don't think my opponent is capable of hurting me."

"There's a difference between being fearless and being arrogant," Andre said. "The arrogant person is someone who deludes himself into thinking he's so good he doesn't need to prepare. But that's false bravado. That's trying to hide from fear. It doesn't work.

"It's important to define fear properly: Fear is the strong, unpleasant emotion that *expects* something bad to happen. If a fighter doesn't train hard and prepare for his opponent, then he can rightly expect bad things to happen in the ring. You *should* be full of fear if you haven't properly prepared for something. On the other hand, proper preparation and hard training should eliminate fear.

"It's like the kid who thinks he's so smart he doesn't need to study for the test. That's not being fearless; that's being arrogant. Only if the kid puts in the hours to study can he walk into test day with the fearless confidence that helps him ace the test. Preparation eliminates fear.

"The guy who thinks he doesn't need to prepare isn't fearless, he's delusional. The fighter who doesn't prepare for his opponent *should* be afraid. Only the fighter who has thoroughly prepared has earned the right to be fearless.

"Action and preparation conquer fear. We will train away your fear."

"But isn't it important to listen to your fears?" I asked. "Don't your fears tell you when you should or should not do something?"

"Your instincts tell you when something is dangerous," Andre said. "But that's not the same as fear. Your instincts tell you not to cross the street in heavy traffic. You don't need the emotion of fear to tell you that.

"You see, fear is an emotion. A very powerful emotion. Often times, we hear people talk about fears and instincts as if they're the same, but they're not.

"Again, let's make sure we properly define fear. Fear is the strong, unpleasant emotion that *expects* something bad to happen. Your instinct is your alert system that tells you to do or not do something based on past events—either learned or experienced. Instincts are good for you; fears are not."

Andre was making me see fear in a new way. I was one of those people who thought listening to your fears and listening to your instincts were the same thing. I had been taught by my previous trainer that fear was good for me.

"You're saying fear won't make me a sharper, more dangerous fighter?" I asked.

Andre shook his head. "It's just the opposite. The fearless fighter will always be sharper and more dangerous than the fear*ful* fighter. The fighter full of fear will be tight, timid, and indecisive because he'll be overthinking everything—afraid to trust his instincts. The fearless fighter will be confident—he'll be able to let go and trust his instincts in the ring. Once that bell rings, you need to be fearless."

"And you think I'm a fearful fighter?"

"I do. And we're going to change that. **Fear is the biggest, baddest opponent you will ever face. Until you win the fight against fear, you'll never win the fight in the ring.**"

"And how do I win the fight against fear?"

"You approach it just like any other opponent. The first thing you have to do is recognize it. A fighter can't dodge or block a punch he doesn't see coming. It's the same with fear. **You have to identify exactly what it is you fear before you can defeat it.**

"I watch you in your fights and I see that you're afraid of something big. What are you thinking about in that ring? What is the exact fear holding you back?"

"Fear of failure, I guess. I don't want to screw up. I don't want to lose."

"Fear of failure is too vague," Andre said. "*Every* fear is ultimately a fear of failure. You have to determine *why* you're afraid of failing. What are the consequences of failure that scare you? Dig deeper. What is it you're really afraid of? *Why* are you afraid of failing?"

As I thought about it, I could feel the fear twisting in my stomach. I imagined the consequences of another defeat. Would that be the end of my career *again*? Would Andre keep training me if I lost *another* fight?

Memories of messing up in the ring rushed back into my mind. I saw myself getting hit with the exact punch Marco told me to watch out for. I saw Marco rolling his eyes and shaking his head at me. "What's your problem?" he would ask me. "Why can't you fight the way I tell you to fight?"

I thought of all those people who said I was crazy for trying to be a boxer. I saw them smirking about my dream. I envisioned them laughing when they heard about me losing another fight.

I saw myself walking around with a black eye and a swollen face, everyone I passed shaking their head and making some joke about how it's not against the rules to duck.

Then I saw myself searching for a new job, a new career, something that had nothing to do with boxing. A career I didn't want.

All the while, I heard voices saying, "I told you so." I saw Marco laughing, my old football coach laughing, friends shaking their heads and saying, "I hope you learned your lesson." The lesson being not to chase stupid dreams, I suppose.

"You want to know what I'm afraid of?" I finally blurted out to Andre. "I'm afraid of proving everybody right. I'm afraid of losing another fight and having to listen to all those people who told me what an idiot I was for trying to be a pro boxer. Everyone who said I didn't belong in this sport. I'm afraid of having everyone who said this was such a silly dream laughing at me and telling me what a waste of time it was. I've heard enough of that and I don't want to hear it again. But that's exactly what's going to happen if I lose."

Andre leaned back and let my words hang in the air. He smiled big and said, "That's good."

"How is that good?"

"You just identified the exact fear that is eating away at you. And it's one of the most destructive fears there is: the fear of what other people think. I can show you how to beat it."

★★★ 5 ★★★
FAITH VS. FEAR

"Before we get into how to defeat a specific fear, you have to understand what a dangerous opponent fear is," Andre said. "Most people don't realize there's a battle against fear taking place inside of them. They certainly don't realize all the damage fear is doing in their lives. Fear ruins people's lives.

"Your fight against fear is the most important fight of your life and the last thing you want to do is underestimate just how powerful fear is. Fear is the most devastating opponent you will ever face."

"You make it sound like fear is evil," I said.

"It is. When negative things are going on, dig deep enough and you'll usually find fear as the root cause — either your fear or someone else's fear. Fear is the driving force behind all the hate, negativity, anger, and sadness in this world. **Fear may not be the *sole* cause of every negative situation, but it always**

makes the situation worse, and it will always make the situation last longer.

"Fear is the source of all your stress and every worry that keeps you up at night. Fear takes any obstacle that life hands you and makes it bigger. It takes a loss—any type of setback—and amplifies it. Fear makes *everything* worse. Fear will drag you down and make every problem harder to recover from."

"And I suppose that includes losing boxing matches?" I said.

"No doubt about it. Luckily, I learned early in my career just how devastating fear can be for a fighter. I later learned how devastating it can be for every other aspect of life. The fighter who is fearful of getting blindsided in the ring is no different than the salesman fearful of blowing his next sales call, the speaker fearful of giving his next speech, or the entrepreneur who fears losing his business. The emotions are the same. No matter what your goal is, the fear of failing to achieve that goal is driven by the same, powerful emotion. The more important the goal is, the bigger the fear is.

"You will never achieve any important goal until you first defeat the fear that stands between you and

that goal—the fear that tells you, 'Don't go for it, it's too risky, you're not good enough.'"

"If fear is so powerful, how can it be stopped?" I asked.

Andre smiled. "Luckily for all of us, there's a powerful countering force on the other side of fear. Fear is an emotion created by your beliefs and expectations. So is faith. The battle against fear is a battle between fear and faith.

"Remember the definition of fear: Fear is the strong, unpleasant emotion that expects something bad to happen. Well, faith is the opposite. Faith is the strong, pleasant emotion that expects something *good* to happen. These two emotions are inside you, competing against each other. The emotion you choose to feed most will win. **How do you feed your emotions? With self-talk.**

"It's just like boxing. You can dance around the ring and avoid everything your opponent throws at you, but you can't run and dodge forever. To win the fight you have to eventually counter your opponent's punches with punches of your own. You defeat fear the same way. When you hear the voice of fear talking, you have to counter it with faith. You have to repeat statements of faith over and over again in order to drown out the voice of fear. That's how you feed your faith and defeat your fears—by taking control of the way you talk to yourself."

"Sounds simple enough," I said.

"Simple, but not easy," Andre said. "For some reason, it's a lot easier to let the voice of fear have its way. That's the default we fall into. Maybe it's because we're bombarded by messages that stoke our fears twenty-four-seven. Media and marketing companies know that fearful messages get attention. They know fear sells.

"It's sad because all that fear only makes things worse. Think about it; fear is the reason why people do evil and self-destructive things. Nobody wakes up one morning thinking, 'How can I ruin someone's life today?' Instead, they let their fears run wild. They act out of desperation. They feed their fears, they live in fear, then they act out of fear. They let fear control them. **If people would stop feeding their fears and start feeding their faith, the world would be a much happier place.**

"Fear negatively affects everything: our work life, our home life, our families, our culture. Everything."

"Sounds to me like fear is more powerful than faith," I said.

"Actually, we get to decide which side is more powerful," Andre said. "*You* get to decide which voice wins the battle. And you decide by choosing which voice to feed. **Fear can't control you if you don't let it. You can *choose* to counter fear with faith. *You're* in control.**

"That's why I don't agree with coaches or business leaders who try to motivate by fear. All that does is feed your fear, making it bigger and stronger.

"Acknowledge fear, yes. Just like any other opponent or obstacle, you can't pretend it doesn't exist. But don't feed the voice of fear. Don't let your fears get bigger. Don't let fear consume you. It will destroy you if you keep feeding it."

"And you think I've been doing that?" I asked.

"I do. I see it in your eyes. I see it in how you move in the ring. **Being in a state of fear makes you tight, timid, and indecisive. It makes you so afraid of messing up that you never let go and trust your instincts. You can't perform at your best when you're operating in a state of fear.**"

This was the second time Andre had described

fearful fighters as *tight, timid,* and *indecisive.* Each time he said those words, they struck a chord with me. In the ring, I was so afraid of messing up or forgetting something Marco told me that I always felt like my arms were restricted. I was afraid to unleash them and do something reckless. I didn't want to throw power shots because I might miss. I didn't want to go low because my opponent might go high. I didn't want to get in close because my opponent might catch me with an uppercut. I was always envisioning *negative* consequences. I was overthinking everything.

Tight, timid, indecisive. Unfortunately, those words described my fighting style perfectly.

"It's been said that **what you fear is what you create,**" Andre said. **"This is because the things you focus on most tend to become your reality.** Fear is a powerful emotion, but so is faith. Faith believes in a positive future. Fear believes in a negative future. The emotion you give more power to ends up becoming your reality.

"All my life, I've seen this concept play out—in and out of the boxing ring. The emotion you feed most tends to become your reality.

"If a basketball player steps to the free-throw line

petrified of missing his free throw, what do you think will happen?"

"He'll probably be too nervous to make the shot," I said.

"Exactly. And if a salesman is so afraid of not making a sale that he exudes desperation, do you think he'll make the sale?"

"No."

"Right again. And if someone interviewing for a dream job is so fearful of *not* getting the job, do you think that person will interview well or do you think the company will go with the person who portrayed confidence and optimism?"

"I think I get the point," I said.

"Good, because it's the same thing in boxing. If a fighter goes into a fight scared to death of making a mistake and getting knocked out, what do you think is likely to happen?"

"He'll probably get knocked out," I said, knowing firsthand how true this was.

Andre nodded. "Exactly. **Most battles are won before they are ever fought. The guy who is so afraid of all the bad things that might happen is probably going to experience a lot of bad things. But the guy** who has the faith that he can withstand the bad things that happen and counter them with good things—well, that guy is probably going to experience a lot of good things.

"**The more powerful the emotion, the more likely it becomes reality.** This happens because a powerful emotion will drive everything you do—all the actions you take, the words you speak, the decisions you make, and the thoughts you think.

"**Everything you do is ultimately rooted in either faith or fear. When you feed your fear, bad things tend to happen. When you feed your faith, good things tend happen.** It's really that simple."

As Andre spoke, I could feel his passion. It was contagious. I could see why he had become so popular as a motivator. He spoke from the heart. He spoke from hard-won experience.

"It's important to remember that both faith and fear live in the unknowable future," Andre said. "Neither is reality at the moment. **Both faith and fear are nothing more than the *beliefs* you have about your future. Fear makes you *afraid* of what the future might bring. Faith makes you *excited* about what the future might bring.**

"When you approach the day in fear of all the bad

things that might happen, you're going to be timid and you're going to doubt your abilities. You'll go through the day feeling bad about yourself, like you have no control over anything that happens. You'll go around dreading what life might throw at you next — you'll procrastinate and you'll be afraid to make decisions.

"However, when you approach the day in faith, believing that you have the power to go out and make things go your way, what happens? You get a lot more done. You believe in yourself. You trust your instincts and abilities. You feel good about yourself. You make confident decisions. You start making things happen *for* you instead of letting things happen *to* you. You get excited to see what's next.

"Fear feeds all the negative qualities that make you feel bad about yourself: self-doubt, self-hatred, and despair. Faith feeds all the positive qualities that make you feel good about yourself: self-confidence, self-love, and hope.

"**When you choose faith over fear, you create a positive destiny for yourself.** This is why I like to say, **Victory favors the fearless.**"

I nodded as Andre spoke. The way he described

fear, I could see how I had been letting it control me. I had been heading into every fight, every training session, and every day with thoughts of fear running through my head. Fear of failing. Fear of getting laughed at. Fear of whether I had made the right decision leaving college. Fear of what Marco would say if I made a mistake. Fear of letting down my wife.

I was starting each day with the fearful dread that something bad was going to happen instead of believing I could make something good happen. I was letting fear dictate all my thoughts, actions, and decisions. I was living in fear without even realizing it.

Where was my passion? Where were the thoughts of victory and glory? Where was the excitement for what I might achieve instead of the fear of what I might fail at?

"I'm tired of letting fear control me," I said, almost unaware that I had said it out loud.

"That's what I like to hear," Andre said. "Let's start by beating the biggest fear you're dealing with right now: the fear of what other people think."

★★★ 6 ★★★
THE FEAR OF WHAT OTHER PEOPLE THINK

Andre decided we might as well get in some road work as we talked about the fear I was struggling with. We started on a run through the quiet, hilly backroads that surrounded his property.

"We've got to do something about your fear of what others think." Andre said as we trotted side-by-side on a cool, misty afternoon. **"It's hard enough dealing with whatever adversity life throws your way. You only make it worse by worrying about what the critics will think of you."**

"I don't know how I got this way," I said. "I used to take pride in not caring about what others thought. It's why I made the decision to pursue this career in the first place. I did it *despite* what everyone else thought I should do. Now, I can't stop thinking that everyone else must have been right."

"I've seen this fear hold many people back," Andre said. "It's one we all must learn to defeat.

"Let's start by figuring out exactly when this became a fear for you. You say you used to not care what others thought. When did that change?"

I thought about it for a moment as we jogged and said, "I guess it was shortly after I decided to become a pro boxer. People were telling me what a bad idea it was. I could tell even my trainer, Marco, thought it was silly. I started wondering if they were right. I trained hard and I was motivated, but in the back of my mind I couldn't shake the worry that maybe I *was* being irresponsible for chasing this dream."

Andre nodded. "Makes perfect sense. You were doing something different, something the rest of the world thinks is impractical. After the initial excitement of deciding to pursue your dream, the reality of what a long and difficult road it was going to be set in. And you had naysayers jumping at the chance to reinforce doubts in your mind."

"Exactly," I said, starting to get a little winded.

"Any time you chase a big dream, there are going to be critics and naysayers telling you not to," Andre said. "That's how you know it's a worthy dream.

Critics want to lock you into paths that fit their expectations for you. And I've got news for you — you'll *never* win over those critics. You could be undefeated right now and you'd have those same people trying to derail your dream, saying you haven't fought anybody yet, saying you got lucky, saying you need to get a real job because the odds are so stacked against you.

"Critics will never stop criticizing you because they can't stand the idea of someone they know chasing their dream and succeeding. It makes them question themselves. It makes them wonder what they could have been if they'd taken the risk and tried something different. And they hate to think about that."

Even with a bad hip, Andre glided along with an easy-looking stride as we worked our way up an inclining road.

"Don't let other people's opinions determine your goals and dreams," Andre said. "**It doesn't matter what anyone else thinks about you. It only matters what *you* think about you. Only you know if you're giving your personal best and becoming the best *you* that you can be. No one else can possibly know that, so their opinions shouldn't matter to you.**"

The road leveled out and there were now thick woods on both sides of us. This was the perfect place to run, surrounded by nature and free from distractions.

"It's hard to ignore critics I come into contact with every day," I said. "These are friends and people I work with. These voices are *everywhere*. Everyone at Marco's gym thought I didn't belong in boxing."

"First off, you need to realize people aren't thinking about you as much as you think they are," Andre said with a smile. "Whether we're talking about friends, coworkers, competitors, reporters, or anyone else who makes demeaning comments about you, once you're out of sight, you're out of mind. People have enough problems of their own. They don't have time to be worrying about yours."

Andre's words cut my ego down to size and I immediately felt...*better*. It was silly to think dozens of people were obsessing over whether *I'd* make it as a boxer, but that's how I felt at times — those times when I was doubting myself.

"Secondly," Andre continued, "if proving yourself to critics is the driving force behind your decisions, you'll never be successful. Why? Because there will *always* be critics you can't satisfy. Trust me, I went through this.

"Anyone who has accomplished anything of note will tell you that you can never satisfy the critics. People said I wasn't good enough when I was just getting started. They said it when I was climbing up the ranks. They even said it when I won a world title — claiming the division wasn't as good as it used to be.

"No matter how successful you are, there will always be people who think they know better than you. There will always be naysayers who try to put you down and people who want to see you fail. No matter how successful you are, there will always be people you can't win over, so stop trying to. **Trying to please critics will only hold you back from reaching *your* potential.**"

I was lucky to have a guy with Andre's perspective training me. He started at the bottom and rose to the top. Then, he got knocked from the top of one profession and had to start over in another. Because he was such a hero around here, I assumed people always adored him, but I could tell as he spoke that he'd dealt with way more critics than I ever realized. It's easy to assume there are people out there who never have to deal with the problems you're dealing with, but that just isn't true. *Everyone* has problems they're dealing with behind the scenes.

"After the car wreck that ended my career, there were a lot of nice things said about me," Andre said as we began up another incline, this one steeper than the last. "But there were also people who said I must have been speeding, I must have been partying, I must have been drinking. None of those things were true. These people said I was getting what I deserved. It hurt me to hear that, but I realized it was coming from jealous people who like to see others fail. **A lot of people in this world love to see others get knocked down because it validates their decision to not go for something special — to not chase their dreams.** They want to be able to say, 'See, that guy went for his dreams and it didn't work out so great after all.' It validates their decision to stay on the sidelines in life.

"I remember telling people I was going to college after my accident and seeing the look on their faces. 'You? College? You don't have the brains for college.'

"I remember starting my first business, giving my first speech, writing my first book. Every single time there were critics lined up to tell me what a foolish idea it was, how the odds of being successful were so slim, how it was all such a waste of time.

"It's kind of funny when you think about, Mickey. All the things critics said *you* should be doing—going to college, starting a career—are things they said *I* shouldn't be doing. They said you didn't belong in boxing; they said I didn't belong outside of boxing.

"The world is full of people who will find the negative in every situation. You will never be good enough in their eyes. What matters is whether you're good enough in *your* eyes. That's it. That's all that matters. That's not being self-absorbed, that's recognizing the truth. Nobody knows you as well as you do. You have to block out the opinions of others."

"And how do I do that?" I said, now sweating hard and panting as Andre glided along. This was the first road work I had done since being fired by Marco and it was showing.

Andre glanced my way and took mercy on me by slowing down his pace as we reached the top of the steep hill we'd been climbing. We were now above the wooded area we had run through.

"Whenever you hear the critics, remember this," Andre said. **"There are two types of people in this** world: those who believe success is a choice and those who make excuses for why they're not successful. The critics are jealous of those who dare to go for greatness. They're always blaming, whining, and making excuses for why they haven't achieved more. They love to make themselves out to be victims. They cut other people down, hoping to make themselves look better. It's sad.

"Always remember what the critics and naysayers represent. Remember that there are doers and there are critics. There are achievers and there are excuse-makers. When you hear critics running their mouths, remember what side of the line they're on. And remind yourself what side you're on."

I liked what I was hearing. Andre's words made me see critics in a new light. After jogging for a good quarter-mile, I asked Andre about another source of naysayers.

"What about the naysayers who don't want to see me fail?" I asked. "What if they're people who care about me and don't want to see me get disappointed?"

Andre gave another knowing nod. "I call them the doubters. They may not be naysayers and they may not be critics, but they are doubters just the same.

They love you. They want what's best for you. But they don't know you like you know you.

"They don't know what you know. They don't see what you see. They don't know what God put in your heart. They don't have the purpose that you have. Therefore, you have to respond to the doubters the same way you respond to the critics: remembering that nobody knows you as well as you know you. If the doubters truly love you, they will respect that and support you."

We went a little further before I blurted out another source of fear that had been weighing on me.

"And what if I'm afraid of letting down the people who are depending on me?" I asked. "I fear letting down my wife. She's depending on me. My future kids are depending on me. What if I fail and I've wasted my time and money chasing a fruitless dream? I'm not only failing myself, I'm failing my family."

Andre came to a stop and I did the same. I was taking deep breaths.

"**The problem isn't caring about the people close to you—the problem is letting** *fear* **be your motivator**," Andre said. "Remember, fear is an emotion driven by your expectations. Like every other fear, fearing that you're going to let someone down makes you timid, tight, and indecisive. That's what fear does. It stresses you out and eats you up inside.

"This is why you have to ignore the voice of fear and listen to the voice of faith. **Instead of being motivated by what might happen if you let people down, you should be motivated by what might happen if you lift people up.**

"If you're thinking about what will happen if you let people down, *fear* is the motivator. If you're envisioning what you can do to lift people up, *faith* is the motivator. **Fear makes you focus on what you *don't* want to have happen. Faith makes you focus on what you *do* want to have happen.** Cancel out your fearful visions of bad things happening and replace them with faith-filled visions of good things happening."

As Andre explained the difference between these two motivating forces, I started to *feel* different. **Fear as a motivating force feels restrictive and heavy. It makes you afraid of the future. Faith as a motivating force feels freer and lighter. It makes you look forward to the future.**

"It all comes back to that inner battle inside of you,"

Andre said. "When fear tries to talk down to you, don't just sit back and let it keep talking. Fight back with self-affirming statements of faith.

"**When fear says, 'You will fail and people will laugh at you.' You have to say, 'I will succeed and people will be inspired by me!'**

"**When you stand up to fear, make sure your self-talk is always in the first person: I will, I can, I am.**

"**When fear says, 'You will fail and let people down.' You say, 'I will succeed and lift people up!'**

"**When fear says, 'You don't belong here, you don't have what it takes.' You say, 'I am listening to my heart and living my God-given purpose. I have the power to succeed.'**

"These two competing voices are both addressing what *might* happen in the future, but these two voices have much different opinions on how it will play out. The voice you listen to most will be more likely to play out in reality."

Andre turned towards me and lightly punched his fists together twice to indicate a fight between two sides. "**No matter the situation, fear and faith are constantly battling each other. You get to choose which side wins by choosing which side to feed.**"

Andre took a deep breath as he looked upward.

"The fear of what other people think will prevent you from becoming the person God made you to be," he said. "Don't try to be someone you're not. Don't worry about what others might think of you. Don't compare yourself to others. Follow *your* heart. Be the best that *you* can be. Only you know if you're living up to your potential.

"You can win a fight and have people praising you on the outside, but if you know in your heart you didn't train your best or you didn't give your best during the fight, then you need to hold yourself accountable. At the same time, you can lose a fight and hear all the people saying, 'I told you so,' but if you gave your absolute best in training and if you left everything you had in the ring, then you will know in your heart you were the best that you could be. That's what it means to succeed and that's why *your* honest opinion is the only opinion that matters.

"**Don't give your power to anyone else. Your only goal should be to become the best version of *you*, not the best version of somebody else**.

"Whenever you find yourself worrying about what others think, counter the fear by saying, '**I can't** control what others think, all I can control is what *I* think. I will be the very best *me* that I can be. That's all I can control.'

"As long as you're doing the right thing and giving the very best that you can, who cares what anybody else thinks?"

"Right," I nodded. "Who cares?"

"Of course, this doesn't mean you shut out *all* outside opinions and advice," Andre said. "You want to learn from those who want to help you succeed. You want to listen to those who are capable of helping you become the very best you can be."

I knew what Andre was getting at and gave him a sarcastic smile. "And let me guess, you're one of those people I should be listening to?"

He laughed. "Yes, indeed. And my opinion is that your conditioning needs some serious improvement. Let's get moving."

We started jogging again and I felt lighter. The heavy fear of what other people thought slowly lifted off my back as I ran.

Over the next several weeks, every time I replayed a snarky comment or envisioned people laughing at me, I immediately asked myself, *Am I giving my best?*

Am I becoming the best that I can be? Am I chasing my dream? If I am, then who cares what anyone else thinks?

These questions shifted the power from *them* to *me*. It reminded me that only I know if I'm giving my best. Only I know if I'm chasing the dream in my heart. If I know I'm giving *my* best and chasing *my* dream, that is all that matters.

The opinions of others slowly lost their power over me.

It didn't matter what anyone else thought of me. It only mattered what *I* thought of me.

ROUND ONE

Patterson vs. McGavin
ROUND 1…

In most boxing matches, each fighter will settle into a role as either the attacker or the reactor, the brawler or the dodger, the puncher or the counter-puncher. Whatever you want to call it, the fighter on offense brings the fight to his opponent. The fighter on defense reads and reacts, counters every move, and waits to strike when the moment is right.

Neither strategy is necessarily better than the other. Floyd Mayweather, Jr. made an entire undefeated career out of being a defensive fighter, utilizing his quickness, dancing away from his opponents while stinging them with pinpoint-accurate jabs and patiently waiting for the perfect knockout opportunity. Mike Tyson was very much an offense-minded fighter, preferring to unleash his stunning power on opponents as quickly as he possibly could.

Most fighters tend to do a little of both. They usually have a plan heading into the fight regarding the role they expect to execute, but depending on how the fight goes, the prefight strategy will often get scrapped and a fighter must adapt into a role he didn't expect. However it plays out, at any given point in a fight, one guy is usually on offense and one guy is usually on defense. One fighter is moving forward and attacking while the other fighter is backing up and reacting.

But every once in a while, you see two fighters who come out with the same offense-first mentality. They both enter the ring in attack mode and refuse to back off and play the defensive game. Neither fighter is willing to concede the offensive role. When this happens, epic battles ensue.

It happened when "Marvelous" Marvin Hagler and Thomas "The Hitman" Hearns fought each other in 1985. The fight only lasted three brutal rounds, but to this day it's known as "The War" and it's considered one of the greatest fights of all time.

It happened whenever Micky Ward and Arturo

Gatti fought each other in the 2000s, marking the greatest trilogy of fights so far this century.

And it's happening on this night when I face Bruno Patterson for the world heavyweight championship.

Everyone in the arena expects me to play defense early. Conventional wisdom says the only way to beat a guy with Patterson's power is to play smart defense, avoid his power as best you can, and let him punch himself out as the fight goes on. Maybe, just maybe, you can survive until the later rounds and then land a knockout blow on the worn-out power-puncher.

It's the strategy Muhammad Ali used against George Foreman in the legendary "Rumble in the Jungle" fight in 1974. The boxing world had never seen a fighter with Foreman's power and Ali relied on quickness, an unnatural ability to withstand Foreman's power, and his famous "rope-a-dope" tactic to let the bigger man punch himself out for seven rounds. In the eighth, Ali pounced on the worn-out Foreman and scored one of history's greatest knockouts. Ever since, fighters and trainers have been trying to follow some form of Ali's strategy when facing more powerful opponents.

Everyone expects me to do the same against

Patterson. It's exactly what most fighters have tried against him. I'm sure it's exactly what Patterson is expecting me to do.

According to the critics, it's the only way I'll have a chance of surviving against such a superior fighter.

These are the same critics who say I don't belong in this fight. They say I'm nothing more than a tune-up and an easy paycheck for the champ. They say this is the final bow for my good-but-not-great career and they smugly laugh that if I don't avoid Patterson's power, I'll leave the ring in a stretcher.

But I can't control what anyone else thinks and therefore I don't care what anyone else thinks. I control what *I* think.

Eight years ago, I stopped caring what others thought of me and started focusing on what I could do to become the very best fighter *I* could be. My career took off when I overcame the fear of what others think.

I'm not going to worry about what others think tonight. I'm going to control my thoughts and fight my fight. If I lose, then I lose. But at least I go out giving my best and not catering to what the critics think I should do.

I will not let Patterson dictate the fight. If I go down, I'm going down swinging.

Andre and I have devised a plan that should catch Patterson off guard. I will be the aggressor in Round 1. I will not let him bring the fight to me. I will strike first.

Seconds into the first round, the two of us are throwing power shots at each other in the center of the ring. Right and left, right and left, the sounds of thunder as our heavyweight blows pound into each other. He lands a hook to the side of my jaw and I counter with a hook of my own that connects squarely under his eye.

Not thinking, just fighting.

Boom-boom, boom-boom. Some land and some miss. Some of our shots slam into shoulders and gloves, some slam into each other's faces. Neither of us wrap up during this first chaotic half-minute of the fight. The roar of the crowd is louder than anything I've ever heard during a fight. They weren't expecting this and they like what they're seeing.

I finally stagger Patterson with a shot to the temple and he takes a few steps back. The first sign of give by either of us.

I pounce, but by the time I close the distance between us, the heavyweight champ catches me with an uppercut to my chin and I back off a step, feeling woozy for a split-second. Just like that, he gains the edge.

Back-and-forth we go like this.

After we both land hooks simultaneously, we separate. I take a big breath for the first time and watch him do the same.

But neither of us wants to let the other man breathe. He steps in and throws a straight right. I lower my head and bulldoze in with a power combination to the body, attacking his ribs.

I back him into the corner and continue on in destroyer mode, throwing hooks to the body until he wraps me up — the first wrap-up of the fight.

He's surprised, he's uncomfortable. I can feel it.

The referee steps in and separates us. After a short pause in the action as we wait for the ref to get out of the way, I go in strong again, but Patterson catches me with a stiff left jab to the center of my face. My eyes blur with water and I stumble back awkwardly. He smells blood and now I'm the one backing up as the champ charges in.

Next thing I know, I feel the ropes behind me. I'm backed into a corner, trying to protect my face from the flurry of big hooks he's throwing at me.

Instead of wrapping him up, I get in close and push him off me.

"Don't push," I hear the ref warn, but I see that I've surprised Patterson with my strength. I've sent a message: *I'm stronger than you realize and I will not be intimidated.*

I step to the right and for a moment or two, we both dance around each other, sizing one another up, catching our breath. Then, at the exact same moment, we both go back into aggressor mode and we're in the center of the ring brawling just like we were at the start of the round.

Fists are flying and Patterson finally pulls back, putting some distance between us. I catch him with a straight left. I make good contact, but he barely reacts. I move in to follow-up, but he's too quick and pops me with a tight right hook to the jaw — his hands so fast I never see it coming. It's not a direct hit, but enough to catch my attention and knock me off-balance.

I back off and shuffle to the right — trying to put

some distance between us while he tries to close in on me.

Back-and-forth we go. One fighter pouncing, then the other countering.

I finally hear what sounds like two pieces of wood clanking together outside the ring. It's the ten-second warning, indicating there are ten seconds left in the round.

The sound brings relief, but I tell myself to finish strong. Patterson must be telling himself to do the same because we both start throwing wild power shots as fast as we can in the center of the ring. Again, some of these shots are hitting shoulders and gloves, but a few are slipping through and doing damage.

The bell rings. The first round is over.

I exhale and the crowd gives us a roaring ovation as we head back to our corners.

I've just fought the greatest round of my life and Patterson barely budged.

But neither did I.

I feel like I've just fought ten rounds, not one. My shoulders burn. There's no way I can keep this pace up. I'm exhausted.

I reach my corner and Andre says with a smile,

"Great job, great job. Look at him, he's exhausted."

8

THE FEAR OF CHANGE

SEVEN YEARS EARLIER...

I won my first five fights with Andre training me, which improved my record to 7-3-1. For the first time since turning pro, I had a winning record and I was fighting with confidence. With Andre in my corner, we were also starting to generate some local publicity and crowds were growing with each of my fights.

Up to that point, however, my opponents had been either young, unproven fighters or past-their-prime journeymen with losing records. Finally, it was time to take the next step and go up against a proven winner.

The twelfth fight of my career was against an up-and-coming cruiserweight with a 10-1-1 record. The guy was generating buzz and this would undoubtedly be the toughest test of my young career.

The fight also proved to be a pivotal moment in my journey as a fighter.

I had never faced a fellow cruiserweight with so much speed and quickness. Throughout our fight, he danced away from me while stinging me with well-timed jabs. For seven rounds, fans booed their disapproval while I awkwardly chased my opponent around the ring. He never did any real damage to me, but his stellar defensive skills prevented me from landing anything of significance.

In the eighth and final round of our fight, knowing that I needed to score a knockout, I desperately threw wild punches at my opponent and somehow connected with an over-the-top haymaker that sent him to the canvas. He didn't get back up.

I scored the knockout with just 30 seconds left. The judges' scorecards showed me losing every other round in the fight. Had the fight gone 30 more seconds, I would have lost in a lopsided unanimous decision.

The Monday after my come-from-behind victory, I met with Andre to review tape of the fight. I was ecstatic and feeling on top of the world as we sat in the makeshift office Andre had set up in the corner of his gym. As we watched a replay of the fight, I winced at seeing myself clumsily stumble after my opponent as he pinged me with jabs. I looked completely outclassed. I couldn't wait to get to the eighth round and see myself floor the guy.

But after watching the first three rounds, Andre turned it off.

"I've seen enough," Andre said.

"What are you doing?" I said. "We haven't gotten to the good part."

"I know how it ends," he said.

While I was proud of myself for finding a way to win, Andre wasn't impressed.

"Is something wrong?" I asked. "I just had the biggest win of my career and you're acting like I let you down."

"I'm the one who let *you* down," Andre said. "We need to make a change. I've known we needed to make this change for a while now and by waiting as long as a I did, I almost cost you a fight."

"What change? What are you talking about costing me a fight? I won, didn't I?"

"Yeah, you won, but you weren't the better fighter on Saturday. That guy made you look foolish for seven rounds. I'm proud of how you didn't quit and how you took over at the end, but you should've easily lost that fight. You know I'm right about that."

I couldn't deny Andre's point after seeing the judges' scorecards and watching the replay of the early rounds.

"What's this change you're talking about?" I asked.

"I think it's time you move up to heavyweight."

"Not this again," I said.

Andre had mentioned the idea a few times over the last year, but I kept telling him I was more comfortable as a cruiserweight.

"Why are you so resistant to this idea?" Andre asked. "You've held your own at cruiserweight, but your God-given talent is power and I know there's a lot more power inside you—we just have to unleash it. You can't reach your full power potential when you're keeping the pounds off to make weight in this division."

"A fighter should avoid the heavyweight division if possible," I said.

"Says who?" Andre asked.

"Said Marco. He told me I'd have an advantage fighting as a cruiserweight because there were fewer fighters with the discipline to make weight in this division. You get into the heavyweight division and you're dealing with more size, more power, and more competition. He said cruiserweight is a safer, more controlled environment. He said there are too many variables in the heavyweight division."

"Marco never trained a heavyweight. Isn't it a little odd to accept his advice?"

"In this case, I think he's right. As a cruiserweight, I'm stronger than a lot of the guys I face."

"But not quicker," Andre said. "Each fighter needs to fight in the division that is right for him and great fighters play to their strengths; they don't try to be someone they're not. You're a more natural heavyweight. I think you'll have more success there. It's time to change."

I shook my head. "I know that guy made me look slow on Saturday, but for the first time in my career, I feel like I'm on the right track and I don't want to mess that up. Remember, I've won six-straight fights. I think we need to stay the course."

"I think you're wrong," Andre said. "We can't just *stay the course*. That's fear talking."

"How is that fear talking? I don't want to change

just because of one fight. Staying the course makes practical sense."

"Even before Saturday, I saw signs of trouble. Yes, you've been winning, but your opponents have been giving you more problems. They're studying you and utilizing their speed to avoid your power. Winning these last six fights has clouded your judgment and created a new fear: the fear of change.

"You fear making a change will disrupt the success you've had, but that's another one of fear's favorite lies. Fear makes people afraid to change, even if the change will be better for them. **The man who refuses to change will never reach his full potential.**"

"That may be," I said, "but you're talking about a *major* change. I've never fought as a heavyweight before. Those guys are bigger and stronger than me. I'd have to change the way I eat, change the way I train, change the way I fight. I'd have to change *everything* we've spent the last year working on."

"It's important to make changes when life tells you it's necessary," Andre said. "I would never suggest changing simply for the sake of changing. But I do believe in adapting to new situations and playing to your strengths. The way you fight; you're meant to be a heavyweight. The only thing holding you back is fear.

"The change in weight class isn't as major as you think. Lots of fighters make this move when the time is right. Evander Holyfield spent his first years as a pro in the cruiserweight division. He moved up and become a dominant heavyweight champ. Why don't you think you can do the same?"

"Maybe someday, but now is not the time," I said. "I'm comfortable where I am."

"**To achieve greatness, you have to leave your comfort zone**," Andre said. "You have to push yourself. You have to change. It's a hard thing to do. Nobody likes change. People get comfortable where they are and they don't want to risk losing what they've got. But to become the best you're capable of becoming, you have to be willing to do uncomfortable things. You have to be willing to change.

"It's not going to get any easier to change *someday* down the line. If you know you'll eventually have to change, there's no sense in waiting."

"Why can't we just work on making me a quicker fighter?" I asked. "Wouldn't switching divisions be the same as running from my problems?"

"Not at all," Andre said. "We're maximizing your strengths. We're adapting to the competition. Every great fighter has to do that. Every great team has to do that. Every great business has to do that. Think of the business that is stuck in the middle of the pack in their market. If they could adjust their product, move their location, or alter their marketing plan to be number one in a different market, shouldn't they do it?"

"I suppose."

"Of course they should. It's Marketing 101. You want to position yourself in a market you can dominate. Why be average in one market if you've got a better shot at dominating a different market? The only reason businesses don't do that is they're afraid of change. They've been doing something one way for so long that they fear the uncertainty of changing. Same goes for the guy who knows he'd be better off in a different line of work, but he stays in a job he hates because he's afraid of change. People who are afraid of change will never reach their potential.

"The same goes for you. Right now, you're a cruiserweight with heavyweight power, but average cruiserweight speed. That's worked okay for you up to this point. But let me tell you, the guys you face as you climb in this division are only going to get quicker and faster. If you make the move to heavyweight, you'll become a fighter with heavyweight power and cruiserweight speed. And we can start adding more power today—I've got a feeling there's a *lot* more power inside you, we just have to bring it out. In the heavyweight division, you will be playing to your strengths. It's where you belong. Why wait?"

"Because things are going well and I don't want to mess it up," I said, getting frustrated with Andre's insistence on changing.

Andre shook his head. "That's fear talking. Yes, things are going well, but they could be going better. And that's my point. **If you want to achieve greatness, you have to be willing to make changes, no matter how uncomfortable those changes might be in the short-term.** To move forward, you have to be willing to get uncomfortable. That's true in boxing and in life.

"The fear of change is one of the most destructive fears there is. People are petrified by the thought of change. They worry about changes in their job, changes in their family, changes in the economy. They worry themselves sick about all these changes. Most people want everything to stay the same. They will do almost anything they can—no matter how self-destructive—to avoid change. Yet, isn't it ironic that the only constant in life is change itself?"

What Andre was saying made sense, but the thought of changing still made me squirm. Why *did* I have such a negative reaction to the idea?

"I know I didn't look great on Saturday, but you can't deny the success we've had over the past year." I said, continuing to make my case for keeping things the same.

"There are times when success can be more dangerous than failure," Andre said. "Success can make you complacent. It can make you rest on your laurels. Success can also cloud your judgment and prevent you from seeing problems that are arising. You start coasting along, thinking if you just keep everything exactly the same, the success will continue. But right when you think you have everything figured out, that's when you get blindsided.

"I've learned there's no such thing as staying the same. **At any given time, you're either moving forward or falling backwards. Trying to keep things the same and trying to avoid change leads to falling**

backwards.

"Mickey, you're a good cruiserweight, but you could be a *great* heavyweight. Jimmy Johnson, the famous football coach, used to ask his teams, '**Do you want to play it safe and be good or do you want to take a chance and be great?**' You can play it safe, keep everything the same, and be a good cruiserweight. Or, you can take a chance, make the change, and be a great heavyweight. **Don't let the fear of change keep you from taking the risks necessary to achieve greatness.**

"You saw the tape, you know it's time for change."

"What if I change and it doesn't work?" I said. "I don't want to make some big change, then lose and wish I'd stayed a cruiserweight."

"With every change comes risk, there's no way around that," Andre said. "But not changing brings a greater risk. That's what most people don't realize. **It's a greater risk *not* to change when you know in your heart that's what you need to do.**

"I want you to reach your full potential as a fighter. I want you to become one of the most powerful punchers in the world and the only way we can do that is if you move up to heavyweight. As a cruiserweight, your power potential will always be held in check due to the weight restrictions. As a heavyweight, you'll be quicker than most your opponents *and* we'll be able to add as much power as possible. We'll be playing to your strengths. We'll be unleashing your full potential."

"When you put it like that, it makes sense" I said, feeling better about the idea. "But it's still a risk."

"Of course, it's a risk," Andre said. "***Every* change carries risk. You have to ask yourself if the risk is worth the reward.** I believe it is. But it really doesn't matter what I believe. The choice is yours."

I let out a huff of frustration. "Everything you're saying sounds right. It makes sense. So, why is it so hard for me to pull the trigger on this?"

"Because of fear," Andre said. "But, just like every other fear, the fear of change can be defeated. You defeat it the same way you defeat other fears. You defeat it with faith-filled self-talk. And sometimes, simply redefining your fear is enough to defeat it."

"What do you mean, *redefine* it?"

Andre walked over to a large whiteboard along the wall of his makeshift office. He grabbed a marker and wrote: **CHANGE EQUALS GROWTH**.

Underneath that line, he wrote: **GROWTH**

EQUALS SUCCESS.

"From now on," Andre said, turning back towards me, "whenever you hear the word *change*, flip it to *growth* in your mind.

"When you hear it's time to *change*, that can cause fear and anxiety. So, flip it in your head. Tell yourself it's time to *grow*.

"When fear says, 'You should seek safety by refusing to change,' you counter that with, 'I will seek victory by choosing to grow.'

"A refusal to change is what some people call a fixed mindset," Andre continued. "It operates under the notion that there's no room for growth, everything is what it is, and therefore there's no reason to change. A fixed mindset doesn't believe you can change or get better. It doesn't believe you can grow. It doesn't believe trying to change will make any difference. A fixed mindset is wrong, of course, because everything and everyone is constantly changing. *Nothing* **stays the same. There's no such thing as** *static* **success. At any given time, you're either growing or you're dying. Trying to** *maintain* **is the same as going stagnant, which leads to dying — to losing.**

"On the other hand, a willingness to change leads

to growth. Some people call this a growth mindset. It recognizes that no matter where you are, there's always room for improvement, room for growth. Nobody is stuck, no failure is permanent. **To win — in sports, in business, and in life — you have to continuously grow. And the only way to grow is through change.** *Change equals growth and growth equals success."*

Andre turned back to the whiteboard and underlined the last line he wrote several times: GROWTH EQUALS SUCCESS.

"Don't look at change as something scary," Andre said as he turned back to face me. "Don't look at it as something that can hamper your success. Instead, see change as something that is *vital* to your success.

"When you get to be my age, you'll probably find that you fear aging. Most people do. I did. But then I reminded myself that aging is just another form of changing and changing is growing. I remind myself that *growing* older is a good thing."

Once again, Andre had a way of making me see things differently. Nobody likes to change, but everyone likes to grow. And yet, changing and growing are the same thing.

"I don't think it's time for you to *change* as a fighter," Andre said. "I think it's time for you to *grow* as a fighter.

"Whenever fear says to avoid change, remind yourself it's time to grow."

Over the next four months, I put on fifteen pounds and moved up to heavyweight. My first fight as a heavyweight wasn't nearly as intimidating as I thought it would be. Andre was right, I felt more natural fighting as a heavyweight. I was more comfortable in the ring. For the first time in my boxing career, I felt like the faster fighter. I won with a second-round knockout against a much slower opponent.

I would win seven more heavyweight fights over the next year. At 16-3-1, the boxing world was starting to take notice.

But with more success came more important decisions.

9

ROUND TWO

Patterson vs. McGavin
ROUND 2...

"Change of plans," Andre says to me as I sit on the stool in my corner between Round 1 and Round 2. "He's more uncomfortable than I thought he'd be. I want you to stay in attack mode in Round 2. Take it to him."

Our game plan heading into the fight was to come out swinging with everything I had in Round 1. We thought my best chance at scoring a surprise knockout would come in the first round, since Patterson would be expecting me to keep my distance. However, we knew this strategy would be risky because it would deplete my energy. Our plan prior to the fight was to attack in Round 1 and then back off and play more defense in Rounds 2 and 3. We thought this would allow me to catch my breath if I didn't score a first-round knockout and it would also keep Patterson unsure of what I'd do next.

But Andre was scrapping our original plan. And this new plan was risky.

If I stay in attack mode, I'm setting myself up for a shorter fight. A pace like this can't last long.

The idea that Patterson might be vulnerable if I could take him into the later rounds was essentially being scrapped by Andre. Staying in relentless attack mode for Round 2 was declaring a new game plan for the fight: knock him out or get myself knocked out — a game plan all the critics would call crazy.

"Can you keep it going?" Andre asks. "You got it in ya?"

"Absolutely," I say.

When a weightlifter maxes out on reps, reaching the point where he can't possibly hit another rep, he then racks the weight, rests for a minute, and finds himself amazingly rejuvenated. Just sixty seconds after depleting his muscles of all their energy, he's ready to bang out another set of reps. He won't hit as many reps as he did during the previous set, but he's refreshed and ready to try.

The same thing happens in boxing. One minute after burning up my shoulders and feeling like I've exhausted my system to the point that I'll barely be able to go another round, I now find myself reenergized and anxious to reenter destroyer mode.

"Good," Andre says as I stand up in my corner, waiting for the Round 2 bell. "Give it everything you've got. We're going all in."

I nod and bang my gloves together, ready to pick up where I left off.

This change in plans is a risk, but isn't everything?

Working with Andre over the years, I've learned to trust his judgment and adapt quickly. I've learned not to fear change. Change equals growth and I have grown a great deal as a fighter over the last eight years. **To become a champion, you must continuously grow — and you can't grow if you're not willing to change.**

I look across the ring and see Patterson standing in his corner. Fear comes back.

He's not heaving anymore. His arms aren't dangling in exhaustion as they were when he walked to his corner at the end of Round 1. Just like me, he's rejuvenated.

His head is tilted downward, he looks at me with menacing eyes, just below his lowered brow, as if to say, "How dare you challenge me like that?" His muscular shoulders, his massive traps. For a moment, I swear he looks just like a bull ready to kick up dirt, barrel forward, and trample his prey.

He's not uncomfortable. He's not backing down. He's just getting started.

In my mind, I suddenly doubt the change in plans. *What if Andre is wrong? Patterson doesn't look uncomfortable. He looks just the opposite, like he loves this kind of fight. What if our original plan was better?*

"Remember, you're not fighting against Patterson, you're fighting against fear," Andre shouts. "Whatever you do, don't let fear win!"

It's a reminder of the most important lesson Andre ever taught me: **to defeat any opponent or obstacle, you first have to defeat fear. Fear is the ultimate enemy. The battle between faith and fear is ongoing and never-ending. And *you* get to decide who wins.**

Fear is trying to get in my head.

Fear is trying to make me doubt.

I will not be defeated by fear.

The bell rings.

After a brief hesitation in my corner, I rush towards

Patterson and we meet near the center of the ring, just like we did in Round 1.

No fear, I tell myself.

No fear.

We unleash big shots and the thunderous sound of our gloves slamming each other's heads, shoulders, and bodies begins again.

10

THE FEAR OF MAKING THE WRONG DECISION

FIVE YEARS EARLIER...

"I just don't think I'm ready," I said to Andre as we sat outside a corner coffee shop in the Brookside neighborhood of Kansas City. "If I fight this guy and lose, I may never get another shot like this."

"I know I don't have to tell you that's fear talking," Andre said.

It was a brisk mid-January morning, but the sun was shining and the coffee kept us warm. It had been two months since my last fight and I was undefeated in my first eight fights as a heavyweight, which brought my record to 16-3-1. Andre and I were meeting to discuss who my next opponent would be.

At this point in my life, Rachel and I had our first son, but we still lived in a small apartment. I continued to work nights as a bartender to make ends meet. Though I was having success in the ring, Rachel and I were struggling financially.

On the other side of the street I admired the big, tall oak trees and traditional bungalow-style homes that lined the sidewalks of a residential neighborhood. They were nice, well-kept, family-sized homes, but not obnoxiously-large mansions. There was a unique, old-school charm to the neighborhood. I dreamed of someday moving out of our cramped apartment and raising my kids in a neighborhood like this one.

"This guy's tough, he's the real deal," Andre said. "But I think you're ready. Fear is telling you you're not."

I had been offered the chance to fight Alex Brutka, a 14-0 fighter from Ukraine ranked No. 18 in the world. If I accepted the fight, it would be featured on national TV as part of the undercard for a bigger main event. It should have been a no-brainer to accept this invitation, but I was hesitant. I had put off the decision for two weeks and Brutka's camp was getting impatient.

"I'm not afraid of him," I said. "The whole thing just feels a little rushed. I've never fought on TV before. This will be the first time most people see me fight and we really don't know anything about this guy except that he fights left-handed, he's knocked out everybody he's faced, and he's ranked higher than anybody I've fought. Is that really the best way to introduce myself to the boxing world?"

I had only fought one other left-handed fighter up to that point in my career and I'd never faced a fighter ranked in the Top 20 before. Brutka was quickly rising up the rankings and there were whispers that he could be the next big challenger in the heavyweight division.

"All it takes is one little mistake," I continued, "and the world sees me get knocked out. If that happens — if I don't look my *very* best — I might never get another fight of this magnitude. I know it's time for me to take the next step, but I'm not sure this is the guy I should do it against. Why not fight an orthodox fighter? Why not an opponent we know more about? This guy's been fighting overseas and we don't know anything about the fighters he's been facing."

"You're having a hard time coming up with excuses," Andre said. "He's left-handed? He's from overseas? We haven't studied his opponents? Give me a break. We'll train for him just like we train for every other fighter. I don't think your fear has anything to do with those things."

"Yeah? What do you think it has to do with?"

"I think you're feeling good about how well you've been doing over the last year. You're happy being undefeated as a heavyweight and you're afraid to take the next step. You're afraid to grow, just like you were before you made the move to heavyweight."

"I'm not afraid to grow," I said. "I *want* to grow. I want to take the next step. I want to start earning a living in this sport. What I'm afraid of is making the wrong decision. This is a pivotal moment in my career. I want to make sure we pick the right opponent for my first fight on national TV."

"Who did you have in mind?" Andre asked. "Give me another Top-20 heavyweight you'd rather fight and we can set it up."

Andre was calling my bluff. I didn't have another fighter in mind.

"I'm sure we can find somebody who's a better fit," I mumbled.

"The fact is," Andre said, "you can find reasons why any opponent of Brutka's caliber isn't right. Delaying the decision isn't going to make a fight like this any easier.

"Whenever you face a difficult decision, you have to deal with the possibility that you might choose wrong. That's life. Is Brutka the wrong opponent for you? Are you ready for a fight on national TV? These are tough questions, but indecisiveness is a sign of weakness."

"Ouch," I said, cringing at being called *weak*.

"Teddy Roosevelt once said, '**In any moment of decision, the best thing you can do is the right thing, the next best thing is the wrong thing, and the worst thing you can do is nothing.**' It's better to be wrong than to be indecisive.

"**Fear creates indecisiveness and indecisiveness makes you weak.** If you're so afraid of being wrong that you never make a decision, you'll never be a champion and you'll never be a strong leader. **It's the willingness to be wrong that allows you to make good decisions.**"

"I don't get it," I said, feeling as though I was missing something. "I want to be right, regardless of how long it takes to make the decision. How is that a weakness?"

"Being indecisive is a sign of weakness because it

lets fear win," Andre said. "**You show me a weak leader and I'll show you someone who's afraid to make decisions. Great achievers *will* sometimes make poor decisions, but they'll never make weak decisions.** They don't inch forward in timid indecisiveness. Right or wrong, they charge forward with confidence and purpose."

"But it doesn't matter how strong and confident they are," I said. "If they're wrong, they're wrong — and they'll regret their decision."

Andre shook his head side to side and smiled. "That's where *you're* wrong. The fear behind indecisiveness is the fear of what you can't control, the fear of an uncertain future. But nobody can know for sure what will happen in the future. No matter how much time you spend trying to make the perfect decision, you will be wrong sometimes. Accept that. **The difference between champions and everyone else isn't that champions always make the right decision, the difference is what they do *after* the decision is made. Wrong or right, they move forward and adapt along the way.**

"**Fear says, 'Don't move forward until you're absolutely certain in your future. Don't make a decision until you're sure you can't be wrong.'**

"But you see, that's impossible. It's impossible to see the future and never make a wrong decision. **If you're waiting to be certain you'll make the right decision, you'll never make any decision at all.**

"That's what great leaders mean when they say they'd rather be wrong than weak. If you spend all your time waiting and procrastinating on a decision that needs to be made, you'll never end up moving forward. You'll weakly wait on the sidelines until you get run over by someone who did move forward. Hesitating is a sign of weakness; moving forward is a sign of strength.

"You have to counter the voice of fear by saying, **'I will attack and adapt. I will not wait to be certain I'm right because I'd be waiting forever. Instead, I will fail forward and adapt as I go along. I will learn as I go.'**

"That's what it means to be strong. Accept that you might be wrong, but don't fear being wrong. Know that you can adapt to whatever happens. You will have setbacks, but you have what it takes to overcome all of them. That's how a champion thinks."

Once again, Andre was making me see things as I never had before.

"Don't procrastinate," Andre said. "Don't be afraid to get out there and try something different. Tough decisions aren't going to go away on their own. You can't avoid them. Make your decision and move forward. If you're wrong, so what? That will get you one step closer to being right. The sooner you make a decision—right or wrong—the sooner you can adapt to whatever happens next."

"Even if that means losing a fight on national TV?" I asked.

"Hell yes! You're never going to be ready for fighters like Brutka until you start fighting fighters like Brutka. There's no magic solution or perfect timing. If you get in there, give it your best, and come up short, we'll learn from it and we'll adapt for the future. But you can't start adapting until you first start attacking.

"**You *are* going to make wrong decisions. You are going to lose fights. That's part of life. You can't avoid it. The key is to quickly learn from those defeats and keep moving forward. Don't procrastinate and avoid difficult challenges. Attack and adapt.**"

"But what if I lose and I don't get another shot like

this?" I asked.

"That's fear talking," Andre said. "You'll get plenty of shots if you keep attacking and adapting — learning, growing, and refusing to give up. That's true whether your dream is to start a new business, write a book, pursue a new career, or become heavyweight champion of the world. There will be failures and setbacks along the way, but there will *always* be new opportunities. And with each failure, you'll come back wiser and stronger.

"Nobody is going to be right all the time; that's part of life. Get over it. **What you have to do is get out of wait-and-see mode and get into attack-and-adapt mode. The quicker you make your decision, act on it, and adapt as needed; the quicker you will start achieving your goals.**"

"What about the danger of rushing into an important decision?" I asked. "I don't want to rush into something I'm not ready for."

"I'm not suggesting you recklessly throw yourself into a decision without proper preparation," Andre said. "But there comes a time when enough is enough. There comes a time when you must acknowledge that you've gone from being prepared to being afraid. **A**

time comes when you've got to stop procrastinating and overanalyzing, and you've got to start attacking and adapting.

"Nobody will ever be the *perfect* opponent for you. Everyone will present unique challenges. But it's time to start facing better fighters if you want to become a better fighter. The only way to get better is to take on new challenges. Like anything else in life, the more you challenge yourself, the better you will get. What are you waiting for?"

It was a good question. What *was* I waiting for? I basically had two options: keep fighting local club fights against inferior opponents or take the leap and put myself on the line by facing a ranked contender.

"I don't know what I'm waiting for," I said. "You really think I'm ready for this?"

"I do," Andre said. "But it doesn't really matter what I think, does it? What matters is what you think. You can't half-ass a big challenge like this. You have to be all in. If you take this fight, you have to be *fully* committed. You have to eliminate the fear completely or you'll keep questioning the decision anytime something doesn't go exactly as planned—and there will always be something that doesn't go as planned."

"I know you're right," I said. "I need to go all in. I just wish I could flip a switch and be confident that this is the right decision."

"You can," Andre said. "You can be confident knowing that regardless of what happens once your decision is made, one fact remains: **the most aggressive person usually wins.** That's true in sports and it's true in life.

"**What's more important than the decision you make is your attitude and your effort after it's made. That's what determines your results. The person with the most aggressive attitude and the most relentless effort usually wins.** He wins the fight, he wins the job, he wins the sale.

"**Here's a simple fact of life: Most problems can be solved quickly by simply attacking them hard and adapting to whatever happens next. When problems arise, don't sit back and passively hope they go away. Attack your problems with aggression. Aggressively find the solution. Attack and adapt to whatever is going on. Attack and adapt. Attack and adapt. The person with this mindset usually wins.**

"If you remember that, it will take the pressure off of your decision. Why? Because **wrong decisions are**

quickly turned into right solutions when you attack and adapt. It's what you do *after* the decision is made that matters more than the decision itself."

"I never thought of it that way," I said, a phrase I often repeated during my conversations with Andre.

I felt a sense of peace wash over me with the realization that it's what I do *after* the decision that matters most. I had been tying my stomach in knots about whether I should or shouldn't take this fight, but that was fear talking. At some point, you have to just go for it. Then, attack and adapt.

"The time to consider all the angles is *before* the decision is made," Andre said. "And we've done that. I think it's time we take the fight.

"But remember, **once the decision is made, there can be no retreat. You have to keep moving forward no matter what happens. Don't look back; attack and adapt**."

I smiled as I looked up at the bright blue sky.

"What are you thinking now?" Andre asked.

"I'm thinking what a relief it is," I said. "What a relief it is to put the decision behind me and start moving forward. Right or wrong, it's time to start attacking."

Andre banged his fist on the table. "That's what I like to hear. I'll call Brutka's camp right now. Meet me at my place in an hour. It's time to start training."

Eight weeks later, I faced Alex Brutka on national TV. He knocked me down in the third round, but I regrouped, attacked, and adapted. I won the fight with a knockout in the ninth.

Winning the Brutka fight gave me a new level of confidence and opened up more opportunities for me. Over the next two years, I would win nine more fights. Some of those fights were against local club fighters, but three were against ranked contenders. Two fights were on national TV and a third was on the undercard of a major Pay-Per-View event.

My record climbed to 26-3-1 and I rose to No. 13 in the world rankings. I was still a long way from a world-title shot, but I was moving up in the world of boxing.

★★★ 11 ★★★
ROUND THREE

Patterson vs. McGavin
ROUND 3…

By the time we get to Round 3, the pace of our fight has slowed some. For two rounds, the heavyweight champion and I have attacked each other with punches strong enough to break jaws, collapse lungs, and do permanent damage to your average man.

But we are not average. We're two of the top heavyweights in the world. We've spent most of our adult lives training to reach this level.

He's the greatest in the world and I am his worthy opponent.

That's what I tell myself. I tell myself I'm worthy. I tell myself I belong in this ring.

I want to believe it. I *have* to believe it.

Andre and I knew coming into this fight that the

third round would be critical. Patterson has defeated 25 of his 28 previous opponents within the first three rounds. Fighters can't handle his power and hand speed.

I *must* make it past Round 3. If I can make it to the fourth round, Patterson will be facing something he isn't used to, something he didn't expect, something that makes him uncomfortable. So much of boxing comes down to simply making your opponent uncomfortable. Those who are best at attacking and adapting to whatever happens usually win.

I'm obviously not the only fighter to recognize how crucial the third round is. Ever since Patterson won the title, opponent after opponent has tried to *survive* the early rounds with him. They've all tried to avoid or withstand his power in the hopes that he will punch himself out.

They've all tried and failed.

Up to this point, I've surprised Patterson with my strategy. I've refused to retreat. He didn't expect me to come out swinging in the first two rounds. He expected me to dance around the ring after feeling his power and seeing his hand speed. He expected me to back away and keep my distance.

But I didn't. I came out attacking in the first round and continued it in the second.

Now we enter the pivotal third round.

There's pressure on me to make it past three. But I remind myself there's pressure on him to end it in three.

I've attacked and attacked hard in this fight, but fatigue is setting in. I must adapt.

The third round brings more pauses and tie-ups than the first two rounds. We're both tired and we both know we have to be more efficient with our punches.

That doesn't mean I have to back off and dance away from the champ. Throwing power punch after power punch in the center of the ring is not the only way I can try to make Patterson uncomfortable. Even if I'm fatigued, Andre and I believe that cutting off the ring should be enough to keep him off-balance.

It's a risk. We're not certain it will work. I could be setting myself up for eating an uppercut that ends the fight, but I can't allow him to dictate the fight. This is the best plan of attack we have for the moment and if it doesn't work, I'll adapt.

I spend the third round relying more on footwork

than punching power.

Patterson and I are both orthodox fighters. That means we fight with our left foot and left shoulder forward. We throw jabs with the left hand and most power shots with the right.

To cut off the ring means that I will try to own the center of the ring. Mentally, I draw a diagonal line from one corner to the other going right through the middle of the ring. I refuse to let him cross that line.

Whenever he moves to his left (my right), I step forward with my left foot and slide to the right with my right foot. Whenever he moves to his right (my left), I again step forward with my left foot, but this time I take a short step with my right foot and then slide to the left with my left foot.

This sounds simple, but it's a skill that must be practiced for years; it must be hammered into a fighter's instinct to be effective. Andre has spent eight years drilling this type of footwork into me. The past couple months have been particularly intensive. Now, I do it without thinking. It's pure instinct. As long as I don't let fear get the best of me, my feet will move instinctually based on whatever Patterson's feet do. **When you take out the fear, you're able to rely on**

instincts and training.

My goal is to make Patterson move to his right more often than not when executing this strategy. This is because it's harder for an orthodox fighter to land accurate punches when he's moving to his right.

Of course, none of this strategy will work if I can't withstand the punches Patterson hits me with. As Mike Tyson once famously said, "Everyone has a plan until they get punched in the mouth."

Late in the third, I receive my so-called "punch in the mouth." This punch is actually a straight right that lands square in my face. It feels like he has shoved my nose into my brain. My eyes go hazy with water and I feel blood immediately release from my nose. Before I can react, he connects with a left hook to my jaw. I feel a slight buckle in my knees. I wobble backwards as the crowd roars with excitement.

This is it. This is a make-or-break moment. This is where I go down like all the rest of Patterson's hapless opponents.

That...or I make my stand.

Patterson smells blood and he closes in on me lightning fast. He throws violent punches at me as I back into a corner. Right-left, right-left, aiming for my head.

I put my gloves up to protect the sides of my face and he immediately reacts with an uppercut that lands just below my chin.

Again, I feel my knees weaken.

"Wrap him up," I hear Andre yell from my corner.

I throw my arms around Patterson's massive frame and try to pull him close enough that he can't move his arms and throw another shot. He tries to wiggle an arm loose and push me off, but I don't budge. I sense his frustration. The ref yells, "Break."

We do as we're told. The ref briefly places an arm between us and then yells, "Fight!"

Patterson immediately pounces, but I'm ready. I pull back just enough for him to miss with a right hook and with the right side of his face exposed, I land a perfectly-timed left hook that rattles Patterson's jaw. I see his eyes droop for just an instant. He's hurt.

Now it's Patterson who is staggering backwards and I'm the one pouncing.

After the shots I took, my footwork is a little off and I awkwardly move towards him with clumsy punches. He regroups quickly and we find ourselves near the center of the ring again.

He tries to wrap up and I go to the body. Hard.

When facing a fighter who is bigger, stronger, *and* has a reach advantage (all things that describe Patterson in this fight), your best bet is to go to the body when you get in tight. On some occasions, you can score a surprise knockout if you manage to land a direct hit to his liver or if you hit him with a perfectly-timed punch to the ribs just as he exhales. But even if you don't knock out your opponent this way, you can pound the strength out of him as the fight goes on. Experienced fighters will tell you it's the body shots that do the most damage in a fight. The head shots that score the highlight-reel knockouts usually open up only after the body shots have weakened an opponent.

I slam away at Patterson's midsection as he wraps his arms around me. Just as the ref tells us to break, I hear the bell ring.

I've made it through Round 3. It might not have been the way Andre and I had planned and with blood flowing from my nose I might not look like I'm in control of the fight, but by attacking and adapting I know I have the champion in trouble. I don't know if I've won or lost any of the first three rounds according to the judges' scorecards, but I do know Patterson is in more trouble than he expected to be in. Maybe — just maybe — fear has started to creep into *his* mind.

Making it this far is a crucial victory for me. I know it. Patterson knows it. Everyone watching knows it.

Only three times has Patterson been pushed this far in the past and those matches were early in his career. He's being pushed further tonight than he has been in years.

They said I was a tune-up fight for Patterson's next big bout. They said I was a set-up. Everyone thought this fight would be over in three rounds…with me lying on the canvas floor.

The critics questioned whether I deserved this title shot — whether I belonged in this ring tonight — and I have answered those questions.

I'm here because I belong here.

I've earned my way here and now it's time to attack and adapt to whatever happens next.

THE FEAR OF MISSING OUT ON SOMETHING BETTER

THREE YEARS EARLIER...

By the time I turned 28, a young fighter from the U.K. named Bruno Patterson had seemingly come out of nowhere to captivate the boxing world. He was steamrolling his way through the heavyweight division and unifying the belts with knockout after knockout.

Meanwhile, I was now ranked No. 13 with a record of 26-3-1. Over the previous two years, I had fought in nationally-televised fights four times and won all four. In fact, I had not lost a fight since Andre had become my trainer.

Despite improving my record and moving up in the rankings, I was still working three nights a week as a bartender. I hadn't "made it" as a pro boxer. And with a wife and (now) two kids at home, I was anxious to start earning a living from the sport.

Whenever you see fighters on TV, you might assume they are earning big bucks and living off their earnings in the ring. In most cases, you'd be wrong.

The purse you see doesn't all go to the fighter. It breaks down like this. For my first nationally-televised fight against Brutka, I was on ESPN's undercard and received a purse of $15,000. But, that doesn't all go to me—far from it. I also have to pay my training fees (gym time, sparring partners, equipment fees, and so on) for roughly eight weeks of training. Getting to train in Andre's barn-turned-gym made these fees minimal for me, but we had started training some at local gyms in the city for sparring and other specific reasons. I was luckier than most fighters when it came to training costs, but they still ran close to a grand for two months of training. After fees, you have to pay your trainer, which is typically ten percent of the purse, and then your manager, which is one-third of the purse. Because Andre was both my trainer and manager, that meant he earned about $6,500 for my ESPN fight—and he earned every penny of that. Up to that point, Andre had spent nearly four years training and managing me without a dime to show for it.

After paying those fees, I was left with about $7,500 before taxes for my fight against Brutka. And that fight was *by far* the biggest payday of my career at the time. For the local club fights I usually fought in, I was lucky to earn $1,000, which meant I usually came out in the red after training fees for those fights.

My point of revealing all this is to make it clear how hard it is to earn good money in pro boxing. Only the elite-level fighters are able to make a living in this sport.

Most fans don't know this, which is why I would run into people who couldn't understand why I was bartending two nights after fighting on national TV.

So, you can imagine my excitement when a guy from Fox Sports named Jay Wilson called me up and asked if I'd be interested in doing some TV work. He had seen me give a few interviews and thought I could do well as a guest commentator.

Jay invited me to do a "trial run" as a guest broadcaster for one of Fox Sports' boxing telecasts. I guess I did a pretty good job because he offered me a paid gig for the next month's broadcast and then the next one and the next one.

In the year after Jay approached me, I fought three times (winning all three against good-but-not-great fighters) and did six broadcasts. I was now 29-3-1 and on the verge of cracking the Top 10. That's when Jay offered me an amazing opportunity.

"I think it's time for you do this fulltime," he said. "We're prepared to offer you a two-year deal that would pay you more than what you're getting for your fights. I think you could make a career out of this. And let's be honest, you're not getting any younger. You're a good fighter, but you have to be realistic — how far do you think you can really go with a guy like Patterson taking over your division?"

"You want me to retire from boxing?" I asked. "Why can't I keep doing both — the broadcasting and the fighting?"

"Because we're about to expand our coverage," he said. "We need someone fulltime. Maybe you could fit in a fight here and there if you have an itch to scratch, but TV would have to be your priority."

"I'll have to think about it," I said.

Jay shook his head in disbelief. "I gotta ask you, why would you *want* to keep fighting? You'd make more money broadcasting and you wouldn't have to train and worry about getting your head handed to you in the ring. It seems like an easy choice to me. You've had a career you can be proud of, but it's time to think about your future. We're offering you a much easier lifestyle."

Jay was offering me a great opportunity. I again asked for some time to think about it and he told me to be quick because if I wasn't interested, they had someone else in mind—this job wasn't going to wait for me.

It was another big decision that would alter my future. I met with Andre to discuss it.

We met for breakfast at a diner not far from my apartment. I asked him what he thought I should do.

"I'm not surprised," Andre said. "You're good on TV. It was only a matter of time before you got offered a bigger role."

"Thanks," I said, almost apologetically.

Andre didn't show any anger or resentment. This surprised me. Because of Andre I was now the No. 11-ranked heavyweight contender in the world. He had spent the last six years training me and I was *finally* being considered a legit contender. And yet, here I was, thinking about retiring just as I—make that *we*—

were about to make it to the elite level of boxing.

Andre was digging into a pile of pancakes. I had barely touched my plate.

"Any thoughts on what I should do?" I pressed.

Andre shrugged. "You have to do what's best for you and your family. If you've lost your passion for boxing, there's no sense in continuing."

His casual response made me defensive.

"I haven't lost my passion," I said. "I just don't want to look back and regret not taking this opportunity when I had the chance. You know as well as anybody, I can't fight forever."

Andre nodded. "That's true. None of us can do anything forever. You have to go where your heart is. If you've lost the fighter's heart, you have to hang up the gloves. Don't even think twice. You'll get crushed if your heart's not in it."

"I haven't lost my heart," I snapped.

Andre looked up at me, surprised at my defensiveness. "Take it easy. All I'm saying is if you're not *all in* in this sport, you'll not only lose, you'll get hurt...bad. This is an area where it's not my job to change your mind. If you're not all in, you need to be all out."

"You're making it sound like I've lost my courage or something," I said. "I haven't. I know I can go further in this sport. It's been my dream since I was nine. I *love* boxing."

"Okay, so if you still love it, why would you even consider walking away from it?"

"Because I also love my family and I have to think about our future. I'm being offered a great opportunity."

"You've also earned a great opportunity in the ring," Andre said. "If this is about money, you know a big payday is right around the corner."

"It's not just the money," I said. "Jay said some things that got me thinking. Things about how high I can really expect to climb and all the risks involved with boxing. I'm wondering if it's all worth it."

"If what's worth it?" Andre asked.

"All the pressure, all the training, all the uncertainty, all the critics—*everything* that goes with trying to make it in this sport. It's...exhausting. There was a part of me that naively thought once I was winning, once I was climbing the ranks, I would feel more certain about my future. I thought I'd get things figured out and feel less pressure. Turns out, it's the opposite."

Andre chomped on a sausage link as if he'd heard it all before. "Every fighter comes to this crossroad at some point. That moment where they wonder if all the blood, sweat, tears, and yes, *pressure*, is worth it. But I got news for you: *any* worthy goal is going to have pressure. That's not limited to boxing."

"I'm not so sure about that," I said, staring out the window and watching the traffic go by.

I heard Andre set his fork down on his plate and ask, "What's that supposed to mean?"

I turned and looked Andre in the eye. "It means, I love boxing, but maybe there is an easier path than this."

He leaned back in the booth and smiled. "There it is," he said slowly. "I see it now."

"See what?" I asked.

"I see a new fear that has developed inside of you: The fear of missing out on something better. The voice of fear is telling you there must be an easier path than the one you're on."

Up to that point, I hadn't considered that fear might be voicing its opinion on the matter. I had also never considered that the urge to go down an easier path could be caused by fear.

"The fear that you might be missing out on something better or *easier* is toxic," Andre said. "We live in a culture bombarded by advertisements that constantly promise quick fixes and shortcuts. Whether it's losing weight or making more money, you're always being told there's an easier way to do it than whatever way you're trying. When you accept that false promise—the belief that there must be an easier way—it leads to subpar performance. Why? Because you always have one foot out the door—convinced there must be an easier path than the one you're on. This creates a lack of commitment. Whenever things get tough, you look to jump ship. It's really sad to think of all the great things that were never accomplished because someone failed to fully commit themselves to the task at hand."

I didn't like the accusation I was hearing.

"Hold on a second," I said, putting my hand up to stop Andre from continuing. "This wasn't *my* idea. I didn't go looking for an easy way out. They came to me. They offered me this job out of the clear blue sky. I have to consider it. I'm not quitting the fight game because things got too tough for me."

"That's not what you said a minute ago," Andre said. "You said you wondered if there was an easier path. I think this has a lot less to do with the job offer you got and a lot more to do with the level of competition you know you need to start facing."

That one hurt and I raised my voice. "I'm not *afraid* of the competition."

"Oh yeah? Then why have you spent the last year fighting guys ranked behind you instead of in front of you? Why have you been content to stay just outside the Top 10? Why have you been ducking the top contenders?"

I didn't have a good answer.

"You know it's time to start facing the best heavyweights in the world," Andre said. "And I think you're afraid. You're afraid that you might be missing out on something easier. You're afraid that maybe you don't have what it takes and so maybe you need to find a shortcut to the top. But guess what? **There are no shortcuts to the top. To be a champion, you have to do hard things. You have to go through things most people aren't willing to go through. You have to embrace the pressure and break through plateaus. You have to keep moving forward, no matter how**

hard it gets. There is no other way. There are no shortcuts or backdoors to the top. The only way to the top is to bust through each wall that stands in your way."

"And what if I lose?" I said. "Let's say I turn down the TV deal and start facing Top 10 contenders. If I lose, what do I have to show for it? Those networks aren't going to call me up after I've dropped three fights and been sent into an early retirement. You know how this world works. I'm getting attention right now, but I'm one loss away from obscurity."

"Mickey, I can't guarantee you'll win your next fight. Nobody knows what tomorrow will bring. But let me ask you this, did you start fighting so you could one day become a broadcaster or because you wanted to become a champion?"

Andre had a way of asking questions that cut to the heart of the issue.

"Things are always going to be tough in this line of work," Andre said. "The pressure is always going to be building. And if the way you react to it is by fantasizing about how much easier some other job would be, then you're *not* committed. You're *not* committed to doing whatever it takes to succeed. And if you're not all in, you'll get beat by somebody who is. Believe me."

Why *was* I fantasizing about another job? Why *was* I avoiding top-ranked contenders?

"Fear is getting the best of you," Andre said, as though he could hear what I was thinking. "The voice of fear is in your head and it's keeping you from becoming your best.

"Fear says, 'The grass is always greener. There's an easier way somewhere else. Don't waste your time and effort here. Keep your options open.'

"When you hear that voice, you have to say, **'I am** *all in.* **There are no shortcuts, there are no hacks, there is no easier path. There is only one way forward and that's through grit and perseverance. Every day I work towards my dream is a day I get closer to making that dream a reality. Success does not require shortcuts; success requires total commitment. I am totally committed!'**

"You'll never get to where you want to be with one foot out the door."

"Burn the boats, right?" I said, referring to a story Andre once told me about a general who led his troops to a battle overseas. Once the general's army arrived at their destination in enemy territory, he had the boats they arrived in burned at sea. The message was clear: there was no way to retreat. It was victory or death.

"Exactly," Andre said. "Burn the boats! **When you give yourself an option for retreating, you'll never reach your destination.** Once you have a goal you're passionate about, you've got to be completely committed to doing whatever it takes to accomplish that goal and you've got to eliminate all other options.

"With any opportunity you get offered, you have to ask yourself, 'Will this get me closer to my goal? Will this get me closer to becoming a champion?' If the answer is no, then don't even consider it. **If you're always looking for shortcuts or ways to retreat, you'll always find excuses for not reaching your destination.**"

"What about safety nets?" I asked. "Aren't there times when I should prepare for the worst? Shouldn't I make sure I have a contingency plan?"

"Sure," Andre said. "You have to be willing to adapt to changing circumstances. But a backup plan should be exactly that: a *backup* if things go wrong, not a way to avoid doing the work required for success.

"The problem a lot of people run into is that they

set their goals high, then realize it's hard work making big dreams come true. Suddenly, a much less ambitious Plan B starts to look better. They retreat to Plan B not because Plan A wasn't working, but because Plan B looked easier. They lower their ambitions. They convince themselves they don't really need to achieve their biggest goals. They can be content with smaller goals and smaller dreams. This is a mistake because what they find is that going after smaller goals often requires just as much work as going after big goals. They trade one set of obstacles for another. **Lowering your ambition is usually just a way of giving someone else more control of your life.** And with that comes a whole new set of challenges.

"Attack and adapt, but don't ever lower your aim. And don't delude yourself into thinking there's some magical path where everything will always be a breeze. A career in broadcasting is competitive too and it will have all kinds of challenges you haven't even thought of."

That statement caught me off guard and I'm sure the look I gave Andre revealed that I hadn't stopped to consider those challenges.

"Whatever you decide to do," Andre said, "you have to go all in on it. You have to get rid of the idea that some other path will be a walk down easy street. That's the type of thinking that causes you to lose your focus, enthusiasm, and commitment for the job at hand."

When Andre said the words *focus* and *enthusiasm*, it made me think of how I'd spent the last week with my mind racing about doing something other than boxing...and how it made me feel anxious and uninspired. Broadcasting wasn't my passion. Maybe it would be someday, but not this day. I was a fighter. That's what I wanted to be and I was entering the prime of my career. Why would I throw that away? I was passionate about boxing. When I was thinking about it, I was excited. When I was considering another career, it made me anxious. Those emotions were trying to tell me something.

But I still had a lingering fear about missing out on this opportunity. What if I was being too stubborn? What if I was trying to force a career in boxing when I was better suited for the broadcast booth?

"You're right," I said. "I haven't been as focused as I need to be. But I also can't help wondering if maybe the world is trying to tell me something. Maybe this job opportunity is God's way of telling me it's time for something different. Every fighter has to retire at some point. Isn't it important to know when to quit? I'm all for perseverance, but sometimes it *is* time to move on, right?"

"Here's the thing," Andre said. "If you start losing your way in the ring, if you lose your passion, you'll know then — and only then — that it's time to move on. And when that day comes, you'll be able to handle it. God will give you the grace to handle what comes then — and only then. I really believe that. When that day comes, you'll have to trust that God has a new plan for you. But only *when that day comes*."

"How will I know when that day arrives?" I asked.

"When what you're doing is no longer something you're passionate about. And I don't mean for a couple days or weeks when you're discouraged after a setback or exhausted from the work you've put in. I mean when you feel in your heart that the fire isn't what it used to be. When the fire goes out, it's time for something new.

"Has the fire gone out for you, Mickey? Because I don't see that. I look at you and I see a man who is still passionate about boxing, but a man who has suddenly been offered something that looks easier. If you've lost your passion, it's time to hang it up. If you're questioning whether there's an easier path, well, that's fear talking."

I could see the difference now.

"The fire inside is alive and well," I said.

Andre smiled. "That's what I thought.

"You can't let fear distract you. **When Fear says, 'The key to success is knowing when to quit and move on.' You have to say, 'The key to success is refusing to quit and continuing to move forward.' Tell yourself again and again, 'I refuse to quit.'**

"Stay on the journey you are meant to be on. Don't go looking for shortcuts. The journey to something great won't be easy. Embrace that it's hard. That's what makes it fun! That's what makes it exciting. Most things worthwhile aren't going to be easy in life.

"No matter what path you take, tough times will come. But nothing is wasted if it's for a worthy cause. **The hard times will make you better as long as you refuse to let them make you bitter.** Whether you succeed or fail at reaching your destination, it's the journey that makes you a better person. Trust me on this.

"Never let fear's promise of an easier path talk you into quitting on your dreams."

I could see Andre was particularly passionate about this topic. As a champion who was forced out of the career he loved due to a freak car accident, I could understand why. The idea of me throwing away everything we had worked so hard for in order to chase something *easier* clearly fired him up.

"The truth is," Andre continued. "**Every path will have its own rough patches along the way — so you might as well make sure you're on a path you're truly passionate about.** The only way through the rough patches is by not allowing yourself a way to retreat."

"If I go down, I need to go down swinging — something like that?" I said.

"You got it!" Andre said. "Don't defeat yourself by looking for something easier."

It was time to recommit myself to my passion. It was time to recommit myself to becoming a champion.

"I think it's time," I said, feeling a surge of adrenaline inside me.

"Time for what?" Andre asked.

"Time for me to give it everything I've got," I said. "No regrets. I'm in. I'm *all* in. If I go down, I want to go down against the best. Let's take the next step. I'm ready for a top contender."

"Now you're talking," Andre said.

Later that day, I called Jay, thanked him for the offer, but told him I was committed to becoming the best fighter I could be, which would not allow for a fulltime job as a broadcaster. He was surprised by my answer and told me I was throwing away the opportunity of a lifetime.

"No," I said, "becoming a champion is the opportunity I can't throw away."

He laughed at that and said, "Champion, huh? Good luck ever beating a guy like Bruno Patterson."

ROUND FOUR

Patterson vs. McGavin
ROUND 4...

Everyone is familiar with "tipping-point moments" in life. It's that moment when you realize, *my plan is working, things are turning my way, this is actually going to happen.*

The end of Round 4 in my fight against the heavyweight champion is one of those tipping-point moments.

I have controlled this round. I've frustrated Patterson with my jab, I've attacked his body whenever he's tried to wrap me up, and I've continued to effectively cut off the ring, not allowing him to dictate the fight. Each of these tactics make Patterson more and more uncomfortable.

And now, late in the fourth, I duck a wild right

hook of his and counter with a left hook of my own that slams into Patterson's exposed jaw. The crowd "oohs," sweat flies, Patterson's head snaps back. He instinctively extends his big arms, trying to grab me — for a moment he looks like a zombie in a movie, sluggishly moving towards me.

But I don't let him wrap up. I hit him with a hard left jab as I take a step back and move to the right. He stumbles forward and I connect with a right hook that lands just above his left eye. His head wobbles and he plows into the ropes.

This is my chance.

I close in quickly and go to the body as he protects his face. Right-left-right. Power shots aimed at his ribs. If I can just slip in an uppercut, I'll send him to the canvas.

But Patterson is the heavyweight champion of the world, the most dangerous fighter on the planet. He knows what I need to do and even if he's not thinking clearly at the moment, his instincts take over and he pulls me in tight, locking his left arm around my right arm to ensure I can't throw another punch.

He buys just enough time to gather himself and reestablish his fighting stance after the ref has us break.

He's able to avoid any more major damage for the remainder of the round, but I see a cut has opened above his left eye.

As the bell rings, the crowd is in a frenzy and I notice just the slightest wobble as Patterson walks back to his corner.

I don't know if I've won any of the first three rounds on the judges' scorecards, but I'm certain I just won Round 4.

This is my turning point.

Despite the voice of fear trying to distract me, I've stayed committed to Andre's instructions. I've gone all in and refused to waver. Patterson is uncomfortable and I've proved I *can* hurt him.

This could happen. This could actually happen. I could walk out of the ring tonight as the heavyweight champion of the world.

Somebody's going to defeat Bruno Patterson. Somebody, someday, is going to take his title away. *Why not me? Why not now?*

★★★ 14 ★★★
THE FEAR OF NOT BEING GOOD ENOUGH

THREE YEARS EARLIER...

Four months after turning down the broadcasting offer and recommitting myself to boxing, I found myself about to face the world's No. 4-ranked heavyweight contender: Isiah Wheeler.

The fight would be featured on Showtime, it would be the biggest payday of my career, and it would be an opportunity for me to establish myself as a legitimate heavyweight-title contender.

Wheeler was 25-0 and the former cruiserweight champion. He made the move up to heavyweight a year earlier and everyone was expecting him to soon challenge Patterson for the title. Wheeler would be the quickest fighter I had faced since moving up to the heavyweight division.

For ten weeks, I trained harder than I ever had before. I knew Wheeler's speed and quickness would be a major challenge for me—after all, it was ironic that I had moved up to the heavyweight division primarily to avoid fighters as quick as Wheeler and now, in the biggest heavyweight bout of my career, I'd be facing a fighter with elite cruiserweight speed.

The advantage I had was power. I was now fighting at 235 pounds while Wheeler fought at a trim 205. If I could catch him, I'd be able to hurt him. But that was a big *if*. Each of the previous heavyweights Wheeler faced thought the same thing, but he defeated them both.

On the night before the fight, self-doubt crept in. I couldn't get over the feeling that Wheeler was out of my league. Did I really belong in the same ring with a boxer as skilled as him? This guy was born to be a champion. He was the son of a former champion and had been training since he could walk. A guy like Wheeler was *destined* for success.

People had been grooming Wheeler to be a world-class boxer since he was a baby. Who was I? A guy people had laughed at when I said I wanted to be a boxer. A guy who was good…but not great. Certainly not elite. Who was I to think I could go toe-to-toe with a born fighter like Isiah Wheeler?

Those were the thoughts running through my head when I asked Andre, "You really think I'm ready for this guy?"

I'm sure that wasn't what Andre wanted to hear the night before the biggest fight of my life. He had to be getting tired of my fearful responses to each new step in my career. I had been afraid to turn heavyweight, afraid to face Alex Brutka on TV, and for the past two years I had been afraid to face a fighter ranked higher than me. Now, after agreeing it was time to aim higher, I was afraid I might be aiming *too* high.

We were sitting on the balcony outside my hotel room, overlooking the famous Las Vegas Strip. When I looked out at all the flashing lights, I didn't feel the excitement those lights were meant to induce. I felt dread. I felt fear. My opponent—the most elite fighter I had ever prepared for—was waiting for me. My future was waiting for me and I wasn't sure I was ready.

But if Andre was irritated by my fearful question, he didn't show it. "You are absolutely, one hundred percent ready for this guy," he said without a hint of doubt.

"I hope so," I said, a weak attempt at trying to match his enthusiasm.

"That doesn't sound very convincing," he said with a smile.

"I don't know what my problem is. I can't stop thinking that I'm about to face the very guy we hoped to *avoid* by moving up to heavyweight a few years ago."

"I might not have liked your chances against him at 195, but I *love* your chances at 235," Andre said. "He hasn't experienced power like yours. And he's not gonna like it."

"*If* I can catch him," I said. "Back in my cruiserweight days, I couldn't catch guys like him."

"You're faster than you were back then. And much stronger. Yes, he's quicker than you. You know this and I won't sugarcoat it. But we trained to get you ready for that. You're going to cut the ring off and when there's nowhere else for him to run, he's gonna feel your power. Every fighter has strengths and weaknesses. Don't be intimidated by his strengths — let him be intimidated by *yours*."

"He's incredibly talented," I said, doing a horrendous job of focusing on the positives.

"And so are you."

"He's *flawless* in the ring. He *never* makes mistakes. Honestly, I wonder if I'm taking this fight too soon. If I lose, how far do you think I'll drop in the rankings?"

"What the hell kind of talk is this?" Andre barked, finally getting fed up with my negativity. "You're acting like the fight has already been decided. Last I checked, *two* fighters are entering that ring tomorrow night, not just one."

"I'm trying to be realistic," I said.

"I hate that word," Andre said.

"Realistic?"

"Yes, *realistic*. It's a word mediocre people love to use. It's nothing more than an excuse. **What's realistic or not is determined by *you*. It's determined by *your* effort and *your* attitude. Saying victory is unrealistic before you even step in the ring makes you a loser before you even try.**"

"I'm just saying, I need a little luck if I'm going to pull this off," I said. "I'll give it everything I've got, but this guy's been fighting since he was in diapers. He won *gold* in the Olympics. He's in another league than me. If I'm going to beat him, I'll need to catch some breaks. I'll need him to make some mistakes. I'll need some luck. I'll need—"

"—Just stop, will ya?" Andre interrupted my rant. "It's not luck that you need, it's courage. You're more prepared for this fight than you've ever been before and you've got a great opportunity sitting in front of you. The only thing getting in your way is fear."

"This isn't the voice of fear talking," I said. "It's the voice of reason."

Andre pursed his lips and shook his head slowly. He wasn't hiding his disappointment at what I was saying. He looked away from me and said, "Haven't I taught you anything?"

"You've taught me everything," I said.

"If there's one fear I can't stand more than any other, it's the fear that says you don't deserve success," Andre said. "It's the fear that says your fate has already been decided and that nothing you do will make a difference in the outcome. That fear tells you to quit before you even try. That's the fear I hear talking right now."

Andre believed that success was a choice and that the choice to persevere and never give up would *always* make a difference. He had constantly preached that message to me. He believed that refusing to quit was the most important ingredient in a winner. He could not stand quitters.

"I'm *not* quitting," I said. "Don't misunderstand me. I'm going to give it everything I have tomorrow night. I'm just trying to prepare myself mentally for the fact that this might not go my way. I don't want to be a Pollyanna. I'm trying to be realistic."

"How can you give it everything you've got if you think winning isn't *realistic*?"

"That's not what I meant," I said.

"That's what you said," Andre countered.

"All I'm saying is I could use some luck. That's what I'm praying for tonight. Wheeler is more talented than me. That's not an opinion, that's a fact. He's much more experienced than me. He's much faster than me. Those are facts."

Andre took a deep breath and composed himself. "That's fear talking. Fear will never stop trying to make you doubt yourself if you don't shut it up."

He turned to me and continued. "**Your destiny is not determined by luck or fate. It's determined by your effort and your attitude.**

"When you say you need luck, what you're saying is you don't think you control your destiny. You're making yourself a victim of circumstances. You're saying you don't think you're good enough. You're saying you don't think you deserve success. That's fear attacking your self-image."

"What's wrong with hoping for a little luck?" I asked. "You don't believe in luck?"

"I know all about luck," Andre said with raised eyebrows and a smirk. "I've experienced both sides of luck plenty of times. But what I've learned about luck is that it eventually evens out. **Throughout your life, you'll end up getting a fairly-even dose of good luck and bad luck. It's how you *respond* to luck—good or bad—that makes the difference.**"

"Well, I'm hoping for a little more *good* luck tomorrow," I said with a smile.

"Hoping for luck is a waste of time." Andre was no longer smiling. "There's nothing you can do about random luck. All you can control is how you respond to it. That's what you should be focused on. But fear doesn't want you to focus on that. **Fear wants you to obsess and worry about the things *outside* of your control. Fear wants you to think your destiny is**

determined by luck. Fear wants you to be fatalistic.

"You've got to counter the voice of fear with the voice of faith. **Fear says, 'Your future has already been decided and you don't have the luck, talent, or whatever else you think you need to be successful.' Fear says, 'You're not good enough; you don't deserve success.'**

"**Fight fear by saying, 'I get to decide what I deserve. I have everything I need to create the destiny I desire. I have the power to make or break my future.'**

"This idea that you don't have what you need to be successful or that you're a victim of luck — that's what fear wants you to believe. That's a victim's mentality. It's disempowering to think that way. **The moment you start to believe that your actions, your thoughts, and your decisions won't make a difference in your destiny is the moment you've *chosen* to think like a victim instead of a champion.**

"You see, fear wants you to look for excuses. Fear wants you to focus on your competition. It wants you to focus on *their* advantages and how talented *they* are. That's how fear breaks down your self-image. That's how fear eats away at your confidence.

"You need to focus on you — what *you* can do. You

have to believe in yourself and your ability. You have to focus on *your* talent, *your* advantages, and *your* decisions.

"You need to constantly be telling yourself, '*I* have the power. *I'm* in control of my destiny.' Never give away that power.

"The fear of not being good enough or not deserving success makes people quit on their dreams. They see someone else achieving great things and think those achievers must have something special — something they don't have. Or, they blame luck — thinking life's winners must have had all the lucky breaks. But the truth is, a lucky streak will only get you so far. In the long run, those who succeed make the decisions and sacrifices it takes to succeed. I'll say it again: **Your destiny is determined by *your* effort and *your* attitude — not by luck or fate."**

"But let's face it, Andre, not everyone has what it takes to be a champion," I said. "And you know what? That's okay to admit. I'd rather be honest about it. I may not ever reach the top of this mountain, but I've climbed pretty high. And I'm proud of where I am, regardless of what happens tomorrow."

"There it is again." Andre shook his head. "The

voice of fear loud and clear.

"**Fear says, 'Who do you think you are to deserve success? Don't aim too high because you might end up disappointed. You don't have the talent, the experience, or the luck to deserve success.'**

"**You need to be saying, 'Why not me? If someone else did it, so can I!'**

"**The bigger you dream and the harder you work, the higher you will climb. Aim high because your aim will determine your destination.** That's how a champion thinks.

"You limit yourself when you limit your expectations of what you're capable of. **You can achieve anything anybody else has if you're willing to work for it *and* if you believe in yourself.** You have to believe that. You have to believe that you, Mickey McGavin, will soon be the heavyweight champion of the world. Nothing less. **You have to *believe* you're the best before you can ever hope to *become* the best.**"

As Andre spoke, I was getting pumped up. Though we had talked about one day competing for world titles, I had never actually pictured myself reaching that level. I just wanted to get into the conversation, to prove that I could be "successful" in some sort of vague definition. I never really pictured myself as one of *the best* boxers in the world. *Why was that? Why was I afraid to dream bigger and aim for the very top?*

A pessimistic answer to those questions popped into my head.

"Maybe I don't want to lie to myself," I said. "Maybe I don't want to aim too high and get disappointed."

"That's dangerous thinking," Andre said. "**We all tend to become what we expect ourselves to become.**"

"But I *will* face better fighters," I said. "I *will* face more talented opponents. Sometimes you can do your best and still lose—no matter how much you believe in yourself."

"Sure, you're going to fall short sometimes," Andre said. "I know as well as anybody how life can throw setbacks at you and I know what it's like to lose in the ring. Every single loss hurts like hell. I'm not saying if you aim high and believe big, you will always win. What I'm saying is if you aim high and believe big, you will always *succeed*."

"What's the difference?" I asked.

"You know the answer to that," Andre said. "I've been telling you this for years. Success is being the very best that *you* can be. If you believe in yourself and choose to aim as high as possible, you'll reach your full potential — whatever that may be. In the process, you'll win a lot more often than you'll lose. But, if you don't believe in yourself and if you choose to lower your goals and expectations, you'll never come close to reaching your full potential. And you'll lose fights you should have won.

"But this isn't really about winning or losing in the ring. It's about becoming the very best that you can become. That's all that matters. That's what success is.

"Your greatest destiny is not your win-loss record. Your greatest destiny is reaching your full potential. **A man who fails to reach his potential will never experience the destiny he was made for.** You — and only you — get to determine if you will reach your full potential.

"**Nobody ever regrets aiming for the top. Even if they don't reach the very top, they still end up a lot higher than they would have if they had lowered their aim.**

"You have to aim for the top if you ever expect to

reach your full potential. You have to believe you're the best if you want to become the best. Think anything less of yourself and you'll fall short of your destiny.

"Stop focusing on what you can't do and what you don't have. **Whether you choose to believe you can or you can't, you'll tend to prove yourself right.** And how you choose to see yourself is up to you.

"When you start obsessing about your opponents and convincing yourself they are better than you, you'll fall right into fear's trap. Fear wants you to focus on what you don't have; you need to focus on what you do. Fear wants you to focus on why you can't win; you need to focus on why you can.

"The focus has to be on *you* — what *you* can do to be the best *you* can be. If you focus on everything your competition can do, you'll start looking for excuses for why you can't be as good as them. And once you start looking for excuses, you'll have no trouble finding them."

Andre was making me realize how pointing out all of Wheeler's strengths was empowering him, not me. I could see why my comments made Andre angry. All the reasons I gave for why I needed luck or why I wasn't in Wheeler's league were simply *excuses* for why I couldn't beat him.

"The fact is," Andre said, "**what affects the outcome of a situation more than anything else is *your* effort and *your* attitude.** Let the other guy worry about himself. Let everyone else worry about good luck and bad luck. You need to be focused on your effort and attitude because that's the only thing that will make the difference tomorrow night. Everything else is just fear getting between you and your destiny.

"Don't let fear limit your potential. **I can't guarantee that self-confidence will ensure you victory, but I *can* guarantee that self-doubt will ensure you defeat.**

"You can beat this guy. But it won't have anything to do with luck. It will have everything to do with your effort and your attitude. You'll get some bad luck and you'll get some good luck tomorrow night, but luck won't be the difference-maker. It never is. The difference-maker is effort and attitude."

Inside, I could feel self-confidence rising and self-doubt fading away.

My fate is determined by me, I said to myself. *I have the power to control my destiny.*

"Mickey, I don't know whether you'll win or lose tomorrow," Andre said. "But I do know that you *can* win. I also know that victory favors the fearless. If you let fear fill you with self-doubt, you'll ruin your chances of success before the fight even begins. You've got to believe in yourself. You've got to believe you deserve success. You've got to aim for being the very best. **If you lower your aim because of self-doubt, you'll spend your whole life underachieving. You'll never know what you could have achieved if you had only dared to believe you were capable.**"

Andre paused to let his words sink in, then continued, "**You can't control a lot of the things life throws at you, but it's the things you *do* control that make all the difference.** That's true in boxing and that's true in life. You know this. I've been telling you this for years. So when I hear you wishing and hoping for luck, it fires me up. Luck won't make the difference tomorrow — *you* will make the difference."

"*I* will make the difference," I said with confidence in my voice. "*I* have the power to decide my destiny." It felt good to say those works out loud.

Andre nodded and, for the first time that night, gave me a genuinely proud smile. "*You* control your destiny. *You* deserve success. Don't ever forget that. Don't give away your power. Don't go looking for excuses or hoping for lucky breaks. Have the faith in yourself that says, 'I can make the difference. I have what it takes to succeed. I control my destiny.'"

As Andre spoke those words, I repeated them internally. I felt my chest expand. I felt *empowered*.

"The fear of not being good enough is all about your self-image and it goes well beyond boxing," Andre said. "**How you see yourself determines how you think, act, and live your life. Your self-image is one of the most important factors in determining your quality of life.** Don't ever believe the lie that says you're not good enough or that you don't deserve to be successful. **If you believe there's no way to succeed, you won't. If you believe there is a way, you'll find it.**"

Over the next fifteen minutes, Andre and I talked over our strategy for the Wheeler fight. As we talked about all the advantages I had over Wheeler, my confidence soared. For a moment, I wondered if I was getting *too* confident.

"Are you sure all this talk about self-confidence won't backfire?" I asked. "Are you sure I won't become too confident and do something stupid?"

Andre laughed. **"There's really no such thing as being too confident. Too arrogant, yes. But not too confident.** There's a difference.

"Confidence is the belief that you have what it takes to overcome any challenge that comes your way. Arrogance is the belief that you're so wonderful nothing will be a challenge to you. We've talked about this before. Arrogant people get exposed quickly and they back down in the face of adversity. Confident people step up in the face of adversity because they know they can. See the difference?"

"I do," I said. "You're saying arrogant people don't prepare themselves for the challenges they're about to face. **Confident people expect challenges, and then expect to overcome them.**"

"You got it."

The next night, I entered the ring overflowing with confidence. For the first time in my career, I saw myself as a championship-level fighter. Everyone thought Wheeler was in line for a title shot, but why not me? I believed I had the ability to beat him.

And I did.

It wasn't an easy fight. He was the quickest fighter

I'd ever gone up against. But I caught him with a few big shots in the third round. A few more in the fourth round. And in the fifth round, I landed a right hook to his jaw that dropped him to the canvas and ended the fight.

★★★ 15 ★★★
ROUND FIVE

Patterson vs. McGavin
ROUND 5…

I don't know how much longer I can keep this up. My shoulders are burning, my arms are heavy, and my lungs are on fire. The minute between rounds feels like ten seconds. This pace can't continue much longer. One of us is going to give. And it ain't gonna be me.

I know it won't be me because I have hurt the world champ. I know I've hurt him because he comes out in the fifth round and does something I've never seen him do before. He backs off.

For the first time in his career, "The British Bomber" does not charge out of his corner looking to end the fight. Instead, he goes on defense. He keeps his distance and holds me off with his long jab.

It's smart boxing. A fighter with such a reach advantage should use it—especially if he needs a breather. But Patterson has never really done this before (he's never needed to) and his change in strategy gives me confidence. It tells me the champ is hurting. It tells me the champ doesn't like this fight. It tells me the champ is uncomfortable. And it tells me there's no reason I can't become the champ.

I have the power to win this thing. I am in control of this fight. I have what it takes to become the next heavyweight champion of the world.

I've been using this kind of self-talk for months, but now, in this ring, I have *zero* doubt that I speak the truth. I know I have what it takes to do what many said couldn't be done. I believe in myself. I believe that right here, right now I'm the best fighter in this ring— and that would make me the best heavyweight fighter in the world.

I slip below Patterson's long jab and throw power shots to the body. I connect twice, but he quickly wraps me up. I hear the crowd grumble. The first four rounds were slugfests and the fans don't like this change in pace.

The ref breaks us up and Patterson dances

backwards. I chase, but I'm too eager. He tags me with a stiff jab to my forehead and then another to my nose.

I finally slip underneath one of his long left jabs and go to the body again, but this time he wraps me up before I can do any damage.

The crowd boos again and the ref has to separate us.

This is how most of the fifth round goes. I'm getting frustrated right along with the crowd.

I'm glad to know I have the champion uncomfortable, but I also have to acknowledge this isn't the type of fight I expected either. I want to end this thing.

The experts predicted the only way I could beat Patterson is if I somehow took him the distance, but I don't want this fight to go the distance. I don't want to take him into the later rounds. I'm exhausted. I can barely catch my breath between rounds and my arms are quickly losing strength. I want to end this fight and I want to do it with a knockout.

I hold both my gloves up near my temples as I crouch and move side to side. This is known as the peekaboo technique and it's something I've used effectively at times throughout my career. It allows me to get in closer while still protecting myself from a hook I might not see coming.

I move side to side quickly, slip underneath one of Patterson's jabs, and then bull-rush my way inside. This time I don't go to the body. I move upward and throw a tight left uppercut that glances off the side of Patterson's jaw, just missing. I follow that up with a sharp right hook that does land.

The crowd cheers. Patterson stumbles backwards.

This is it. I've got him. This is my chance.

I throw a straight left that lands right on his chin. He backs into the corner and I connect with a solid right hook to the cheek. I throw a left that misses wildly and hits his shoulder, then a big right that is just a bit off target.

I'm one big punch away from ending this thing.

Keep punching, I say to myself. *Keep punching. He's gonna fall. He's gonna fall.*

I throw punches while the crowd roars the loudest it has all night. They smell the climax of the fight. This is it.

Then—a blinding flash of white light. My head snaps back. I hear a loud ringing in my ears. Suddenly, I can't feel my legs. Or my arms. Or my chin.

Patterson has just landed a ferocious uppercut that I never saw coming.

I didn't feel it either. I only feel the aftermath of it.

In a split-second, the fight has changed. My mind says, *Step back, step back*, but my legs don't follow the command the way I expect. I stumble awkwardly backwards while trying to push Patterson away from me.

Big mistake.

As I extend my left arm to push him away, it exposes the left side of my face and opens me up to a vicious right hook from Patterson.

Another white flash of light and suddenly I feel the back of my head bang on the canvas floor.

I hear ringing in my ears and I'm not sure where I am or what is happening. It's like I've drifted into a dream state.

It takes me a moment to realize I'm lying on my back. Then I remember I'm in a boxing ring... looking up at bright lights hanging over that ring...in a fight against the heavyweight champion.

It all comes back to me.

I look to my left and see Patterson's cornermen celebrating. *Where's the ref? Is the fight over? What happened?*

I look to the right and see Andre yelling and motioning for me to get up — though I don't *hear* him. The ringing sound in my ears has now given way to a muffled sound all around me — like I'm underwater.

I roll over, get up on one knee and the ref appears in front of me. He looks to the timekeeper outside the ring and then yells, "FIVE" as he holds up five fingers.

"SIX." I can hear clearer with each second he counts.

"SEVEN."

I pop up. Now standing, I nod aggressively at the ref.

He stands in front of me and continues to count. "EIGHT."

"I'm good," I say. "I'm good!" I panic. I want him to stop counting.

"You okay?" the ref says. "You okay to continue?"

"Yes!" I shout.

The ref places his hands on my gloves and presses me backward a step.

"Come towards me," he says. He wants to see if I can walk without falling back down.

I do as I'm told and I'm a little wobblier than I

expect.

For a moment, I see doubt on the ref's face. I see indecision in his eyes.

"I'm ready!" I shout, desperately hoping he doesn't call the fight.

"You sure?" he asks.

"Positive," I say.

He nods, quickly rubs my gloves against his chest, and the fight continues.

I spend the rest of Round 5 hanging on for dear life.

As Patterson comes after me, I do my best to throw disruptive jabs. They don't do any damage, but they do enough to keep him at a distance and show the ref I'm still fighting.

Patterson lands several more big shots as the round goes on. I wrap up when I can and it's now me the crowd is booing for slowing down the fight.

I take more punishment in Round 5 than I've ever taken in any round of my career. Blood runs over my left eye, making it difficult to see. I feel my left eyebrow swelling up fast. I feel a knot below my right eye throbbing.

Somehow, I'm still standing when the bell rings to end the round.

Patterson throws his hands in air as he heads back to his corner. He has taken control of the fight and he knows it. Everybody knows it.

I gingerly make my way back to my corner. My head throbs with pain.

I can handle this, I tell myself. *I'm a champion. I can handle whatever adversity comes my way.*

I'm pleading with myself to believe it.

"Can you go on?" Andre asks me when I reach my corner.

I don't answer.

At that moment, I don't want to answer. I'm afraid of what I might say.

★★★ 16 ★★★
THE FEAR OF FAILURE BEING PERMANENT

TWO YEARS EARLIER...

After my fifth-round knockout of Isiah Wheeler, my career changed overnight. Suddenly, I became "a serious contender" in the heavyweight division. Articles worldwide declared I would soon be offered a shot at Bruno Patterson's heavyweight title and the purse would be...well, life-changing.

As I soared up the rankings, my popularity followed — especially in my hometown of Kansas City. Up to that point, most people showed up at my local fights more to see Andre Holiday in the corner of his protégé. That changed after the Wheeler fight. I became the city's new "overnight sensation." (An *overnight* sensation that took six years and 34 fights to create.)

I was now the No. 3-ranked heavyweight contender and we set up a bout in Kansas City's Sprint Center against the No. 18-ranked contender. I was a heavy favorite to win and the fight was more of a homecoming event than it was a title-contention matchup. That didn't stop the fight from selling out.

I couldn't believe it. In less than two years, I had gone from fighting in small area casinos and half-filled auditoriums to selling out the biggest arena in the city. I didn't disappoint my fans and scored a knockout in the third round.

This brought my record to 31-3-1 and I was offered a fight against the undefeated and No. 1-ranked contender, Terrance "T.N.T." Thompson. The winner of the fight would be in line to fight Patterson for the heavyweight title.

Thompson was a destroyer. He had a stocky, muscular build and his fighting style reminded many of the great former champ, Joe Frazier. Thompson's fists were like cement blocks, but he also had excellent footwork and the stamina to go the distance when needed.

I went into the fight confident. Despite opening as the underdog when the fight was first announced, I was the favorite by the time the bell rang. That was a testament to my growing popularity, the experts said. And I fought like the favorite.

I came out blasting away at Thompson, trying to prove I wasn't intimidated and hoping to score an early knockout. After I won the first two rounds, Thompson caught me with a brutal right to the jaw that dropped me in the third. I got back up, but I was never the same after that knockdown.

In the fourth round, Thompson knocked me down again. I beat the count and Thompson pounced quickly. He had me up against the ropes and pounded away at will. Just before the referee stepped in to stop the fight, Thompson delivered an uppercut that snapped my head back and knocked me out cold as I fell through the ropes and landed in a crumpled mess *outside* the ring.

It was the knockout of the year and it would be replayed hundreds of times. According to the boxing media, the lopsided loss "exposed" me as an inferior fighter who couldn't compete with the best.

I took two months off to heal and get my head straight. We decided to schedule my return to the ring in Kansas City against an opponent ranked outside the Top 20 rankings. This was supposed to be a "tune-up" fight for me — a way to ease back into the ring after my loss to Thompson. While there was much less enthusiasm than my previous hometown fight, we still had a good crowd at the Sprint Center...a good crowd that watched me get knocked down three times before finally getting TKO'd in the second round.

It was ugly. I left the ring bloody and embarrassed.

In just two fights, I had gone from one of the most popular up-and-coming fighters in America to a boxing joke. "Need a punching bag that still draws a crowd? Call Mickey McGavin." Contenders from all over the country called to set up fights with me. They wanted an easy knockout.

Now 31-5-1, I dropped out of the Top 10 rankings and had to face the reality that I would likely never again compete at an elite level. I was 30 years old and whatever "it factor" I once had seemed to have come and gone.

I took another couple of months off to recuperate and do some soul-searching. After three weeks of not returning Andre's calls, I finally agreed to meet with him. It was time to tell him that I had decided to retire.

"Thank you for all you've done for me, Andre, I

never would have climbed as far as I did without you."

"What do you mean as far as you *did*?" Andre said. "We still have higher to climb. This thing ain't over."

We were meeting at Gerry's Pub for dinner, sitting in a booth near the back. It seemed fitting that the place where Andre first talked me out of retiring would be the same place where I told him my career was over.

"This isn't easy to admit," I told him without flinching, "but it's time for me to hang up the gloves. I've had doubts in the past, but this time I know in my heart it's time to move on. I'm certain of it."

My conviction surprised Andre. He leaned back and asked, "You're sure about this?"

I nodded. "One hundred percent."

Andre raised an eyebrow, studied me for a moment, then flashed a slight smile and shook his head. "Nah, I don't think you are."

Now I was the one surprised. "Look, you said I would know in my heart when it was time to move on. Well, I know. Now is that time."

Andre again shook his head. "I look at you and I don't see a man listening to his heart. I see a man listening to his fear."

I huffed. "Here we go again."

"I'm serious. I look in your eyes and I see somebody trying to fake conviction. I see you trying to be assertive and tell me you *know* it's time to go. But you're covering up something. I think you're trying to cover up fear."

"This isn't fear," I said. "I know it's not ending the way we wanted things to end, but does it ever? We took it as far as we could. I'm too old. I just don't have it anymore. And I'm holding you back. You've got other fighters to train now. They deserve your time. They're the future. I'm the past."

"Let's cut the pity party," Andre said. "You know how I know fear is driving this decision? Because you're making excuses and feeling sorry for yourself."

The truth hurt and I got defensive. "I'm not feeling sorry for myself. This isn't about me. I've got a wife and three kids to worry about. You saw what happened to me in those last two fights."

"You're letting fear win," Andre said.

"You know, not everything is about fear."

"Yes, everything is. **Every decision you make is ultimately rooted in fear or faith.** You lost a couple fights and you feel bad about yourself. You're doubting yourself. You're embarrassed. You're letting all those old fears come back.

"I look at you and I see a fighter who is in the prime of his career. You're stronger, faster, and wiser than you've ever been. The only thing stopping you is fear."

"Did you even watch my last fight? I got destroyed. It's one thing to lose to a guy like Terrance Thompson. It's quite another to get dominated by a guy who isn't even a contender."

"You got beat by fear," Andre said. "You went into that fight afraid that what Thompson did to you would repeat itself and that's exactly what happened. And now, you're letting that same fear force you into an early retirement.

"You fear that a past failure will repeat itself. You fear that if you step in the ring, what happened in your last two fights will happen again."

"You're right," I said. "I *do* fear it will happen again. You know why? Because that's what happens when fighters lose their touch."

"The only thing you've lost is your courage," Andre said. "You fear that the failure you experienced is a *permanent* failure. Well, here's what I can tell you about that. I've lived on this earth for fifty-seven years and I've learned something very important in my lifetime: **Nothing in life is permanent. And that includes failures. Not a single failure I've had has *ever* been permanent. Not a single one!**"

I gave Andre a look that told him I wasn't buying it. "How can you say that after everything you've been through?"

"Sure, there were times when things didn't go the way *I* planned," Andre said, "but when I look back on my life, I see how each of those setbacks were setups for something better. What I thought was a *problem* actually just *propelled* me to something better. Every time I got knocked down—in the ring or out—it taught me important lessons that made me stronger and wiser for the future. Every sudden change in my plans led me to a better plan. Every door that got slammed in my face led to a new door that took me down a better path. Every devastating loss eventually led me to a greater victory—in some way. I believe it's all part of God's plan.

"When I say that no failure is permanent, I'm not saying everything will always go according to your plans. I'm saying that every setback can be a setup for something better *if* you're open to new ways, new paths, and new solutions.

"Everyone suffers heartbreaks in life. But in every situation, those who fight through the fear and the temporary pain will come back and tell you that what was devastating at the time eventually opened the door to something better.

"Every single failure I experienced *always* faded away and led to something better. Not some of the time, *all* of the time. Every problem had a solution. Every failure was only temporary. I wish I could go back to my younger self and remind him of this a hundred times. **Every setback, loss, or failure is only temporary. Failure is *never* permanent. Unless you choose for it to be."**

"Why would anyone choose for a failure to be permanent?" I asked.

"They don't do it consciously. It happens by default if you let fear have its way. That last fight of yours, you didn't lose to your opponent—you're a much better fighter than him. You lost to fear. You lost to the fear that what happened against Thompson would repeat itself. And what have I always told you about fear?"

"What you fear is what you create," I said.

"Exactly. You went into that fight afraid that you were going to get knocked out again and that's exactly what happened. You feared that a past failure would repeat itself. You let that fear run through your head over and over again. Sure enough, that fear became your reality. You chose fear over faith and that's what you got.

"A past failure *will* repeat itself if you choose to empower your fear. A failure *will* become permanent if you choose to quit."

"But Andre, if I lose a fight, I drop in the rankings. That's not a fear, that's a fact. When I lost to Thompson, I blew my title shot, *permanently*."

"Give me a break," Andre said with a laugh. "Do you know how many fighters have bounced back from a tough loss to become champions? The list is virtually a who's who of history's great boxers."

"That may be, but there are also plenty of fighters who never got another chance after they got knocked out."

Andre lifted a finger to stop me. "Do you see what you just did there?"

"What?"

"I just told you how common it is for fighters to get beat and come back better off, and you just told me how some fighters never do. That's fear talking loud and clear. Fear makes you focus on the negative potential outcome. Fear makes you focus on why something good *can't* happen. Champions focus on why something good *can* happen.

"What you choose to focus on tends to become your reality. If you focus on all the past examples of failures, you'll be drawn to living out negative outcomes. If you focus on past examples of successful people who bounced back from adversity, you'll be drawn to living out positive outcomes.

"You get to choose what you focus on. And the choice you make determines your future."

"Hold up a second," I said. "I'm not some dour pessimist. You've taught me the power of optimism. I try to look at the bright side of most things. But you have to admit, some failures *are* permanent. Sometimes you get injured and you never get better."

I cringed after that last sentence left my mouth, remembering that I was talking with a man who suffered a career-ending car wreck just one week after becoming a world champion.

"Sorry, I didn't mean you," I said awkwardly.

Andre smiled. "Don't apologize. You're bringing up a great point, one that I've had a lot of time to think about over the years.

"You're right, when the car wreck happened, it ended my boxing career. The best surgeons I could find tried to put my hip and shoulder back so I could fight again, but it wouldn't happen.

"At the time, boxing was everything to me. I mean *everything*. It was all I ever wanted to do and all I could ever see myself doing. When it was finally clear that my career was over and there would be no comeback, I had two options. I could wallow in self-pity, do the whole 'why me?' thing, and accept that my best days were behind me — that's what fear wanted me to do. Or, I could choose to believe that this was happening for a reason, that the end of my boxing career was setting me up for a better future than I had planned. I could choose to believe that my best days were ahead of me and not behind me. That's what faith wanted me to do."

"And you chose faith," I said.

"Wrong. For about a year, I wallowed in self-pity. I was miserable to be around. I was jealous of everyone and I complained about how unfair life was. Anytime somebody suggested a new career path, I made an excuse for why I wasn't meant to be anything other than a pro boxer. I believed life had handed me defeat—a permanent defeat that robbed me of my destiny.

"Eventually, though, I got tired of listening to fear. I realized that if I had started with nothing and became champion of the world in boxing, I could do the same thing in other areas of life. I realized I had a choice. Everything is a choice. I could choose to keep feeding the voice of fear, which said I was a permanent failure. Or, I could start feeding the voice of faith, which said this setback was a setup for something bigger and better.

"**If you choose to believe that an obstacle is actually an opportunity for something better, an amazing thing happens. You start seeing obstacles differently. Whenever you experience a setback, you immediately start searching for the opportunity that will come from it. You create new opportunities by** *choosing* **to believe that every obstacle is an**

opportunity.

"I've learned that God will not allow anything to happen that he can't bring a greater good out of. I can look back now and say with one hundred percent certainty that if I didn't suffer through that tragedy right when I did, I wouldn't be where I am now. Had my career not ended at the time that it did, I would've probably followed the path of most champions. I would have had a few title defenses and then someone else would've taken the crown and that would've been that. Maybe I would've tried a few comebacks here and there, but my life would have peaked as a 29-year-old super middleweight champion and the world would've soon forgotten about Andre Holiday.

"But the car wreck forced me to reevaluate everything. It forced me to change, to *grow*. It forced me to consider that I might be capable of so much more than I ever thought before. It forced me into a closer relationship with God. It led me to college, which is where I met my wife — never would have met her otherwise. It forced me to try things I never would have tried had I taken the normal path of an ex-champion. It forced me down a new path, a path I know I would not have taken if it hadn't been for my career ending when it did.

"Because I went through what I went through, it gave me resilience, humility, and wisdom. It also made me more relatable to people. They started seeing me differently. They saw me not as someone who had a genetic gift for boxing, but as someone who had to overcome great setbacks in life—just like everyone else. If I had not gone through that, I would not have had the compelling story I have now—a story that led me to such a rewarding and prosperous career as a speaker and writer.

"This all happened because I started feeding my faith instead of my fear. I took what happened and chose to turn it into an opportunity instead of passively believing my best days were behind me. I'm much happier with my life now than I ever would have been had I simply peaked as a champion.

"When your time is up as a boxer, I'll make sure to help you find your next opportunity. But that time is not now, when you're healthy, strong, and in the prime of your career. Had I wallowed in self-pity after my car wreck, I would have let fear win. If you walk away from boxing right now, you will be letting fear win. Much different circumstances, but still the same opponent."

"Hard to argue with that story," I said. Andre's story was inspiring and enlightening, but I couldn't shake the feeling that my situation was different. (Why, after a setback or disappointment, do we all have a tendency to do that? Why do we have a tendency to think *our* problems are so much bigger than someone else's even though reality makes it clear this is not the case?)

"But," I said, "it doesn't change the fact that I blew the biggest opportunity of my career. Nobody is ever going to consider me a top contender after those last two beatings I took."

"The fear of failure repeating itself, the fear of failure being permanent, the fear of missing an opportunity that never comes back — it's all the same fear," Andre said. "And fear is a liar. There's really no such thing as a once-in-lifetime opportunity. You'll always have new opportunities — as long as you don't listen to the voice of fear saying you will never get another chance.

"Here's the key: **when you miss an opportunity, you have to actively go out and create the next one. Don't wait around feeling sorry for yourself. Get**

back up and go find a new opportunity. Take the next shot.

"Like I've always told you, regardless of whether the past was good or bad, you control your destiny now. **When things don't work out as you planned, don't sit around wishing and waiting for something better to fall into your lap, go out there and create something better. Create your destiny.**

"Your future is determined by what you do *next*, not by what you did or didn't do in the past. **Whether you won or lost the last fight, the next fight is more important simply *because* it's the next one — it's the next opportunity.**

"That's true in sports and it's true in life. No matter what failures you've encountered or what problems you're struggling with, the season always starts tomorrow. **Nothing in life is static. Everything is constantly changing. It's what you do next that matters most.**

"You have to attack and adapt. Learn from your mistakes and come back stronger and wiser. Champions move on quickly from failure. Champions charge forward with faith and confidence. They know they will be wiser and stronger the next time, regardless of what happened the last time.

"You're not stuck, Mickey. You haven't lost your touch. Your career isn't over and you haven't missed your best opportunities. Your future is up to you. You have the power to change everything from this moment forward. **Don't believe for one second that any failure in the past has decided your fate. Failure is *never* permanent because every obstacle is an opportunity for something better. Every setback is a setup for something better. *If* you choose to make it so.**"

As I sat listening to Andre, I realized that for the first time in months I was starting to get *excited* about entering the ring again. I had spent too long feeling sorry for myself and dreading what tomorrow might bring. Now, I was feeling optimistic about what I could do next.

"Like everything else," Andre said, "this all comes down to that battle inside you. That battle against the voice of fear.

"**The voice of fear says, 'Failure is permanent, so don't bother trying again.' You have to say, 'Failure only makes me better, stronger, and wiser. Just like everything else in life, failure is never permanent. I** am unstoppable!'

"When you get knocked down—in the ring or anywhere else in life—fear says, 'Stay down and accept your defeat.' You have to tell yourself, 'Get up and keep fighting!'

"Mickey, you get to choose which voice you want to empower. The decision is yours. You need to tell yourself, again and again, '**I have the power to create my destiny. The past is the past and failure is** *never* **permanent. My future starts today and I have the power to determine what happens next.'**"

I liked what I was hearing. It was time to stop feeding the voice of fear and start feeding the voice of faith.

By the time I left the pub that night, my comeback had begun. I was at Andre's gym the next morning and we soon booked my next fight.

Over the next ten weeks of training, whenever I found myself mentally replaying one of my painful defeats, I reminded myself, "**No failure is permanent. I have the power to create my destiny.**"

Whenever I started beating myself up for the mistakes I made or the losses I endured, I told myself, "**The past is the past and there's nothing I can do** about it. What matters most is what I do next."

When pictures of me getting knocked out floated into my mind, I'd feel my stomach churn. But instead of stewing on this negative fantasy, I'd replace it with thoughts of me ducking a big punch and countering with a knockout blow of my own.

Most of all, I kept reminding myself, "**My future is determined by me! It's what I do next that matters most.**"

We all tend to live in our own heads. We can waste so much time fixating on negative things—regrets about past mistakes or worries about future failures. What a waste of time those negative thoughts are.

I won my comeback fight against a Top-40 opponent and then I was presented with a fresh, new opportunity.

Terrance "T.N.T." Thompson was getting ready to face "The British Bomber" Bruno Patterson for the heavyweight title on a major pay-per-view event. The promoters wanted to showcase Patterson's next likely opponent on the undercard. So, the No. 2-ranked contender offered me a match.

The experts thought I'd be an easy knockout—a way to hype up the *next* top contender. Though I was knocked down once early in the fight, I got back up and ended up dominating the later rounds. I scored three knockdowns during the twelve-round fight that went the distance. The judges gave me a unanimous-decision victory and it wasn't even close. Each judge scored the fight with me winning at least eight of the twelve rounds.

After my upset victory, I watched from my locker-room TV as Patterson knocked out Thompson in the third round to retain his title and reinforce his dominance of the boxing world. It was a devastating knockout. Thompson suffered a broken jaw and was carried out of the ring on a stretcher.

My victory propelled me to No. 6 in the heavyweight rankings and though all the experts didn't think I deserved a shot at the title, Patterson was running out of opponents to mow down. He wanted a tune-up fight and an easy payday before the next top-ranked contender rolled in to challenge him. I was offered that shot.

After getting knocked out in back-to-back fights, fear had told me to stay down and call it quits. But Andre had taught me to get up and create my destiny.

Instead of accepting my fate as a fighter who came

close but fell short, I now had the opportunity to fight for the heavyweight championship of the world. It would be a life-changing payday and the chance to prove that no failure, mistake, or setback is permanent...*if* you don't let it be. **We are not defined by what happens to us, we are defined by how we *respond* to what happens to us.**

No matter what adversity we have gone through, what matters most is what we do next.

Of course, the boxing world was only asking one question prior to my fight with Bruno Patterson: If Patterson had so easily defeated Thompson—the fighter who *literally* knocked me out of the ring—what chance did I possibly have against the champion?

17

ROUND SIX

Patterson vs. McGavin
ROUND 6…

I sit on the stool in my corner after barely surviving the previous round. The ringing in my ears has stopped, but I still feel like I'm underwater.

"What round is it?" I ask Andre.

"We're heading into the sixth," he says. "Are you okay to continue?" This is the third time he's asked me that question.

I nod.

My head is throbbing. There's no way to hold it that doesn't hurt. It's hard to think. I'm exhausted from head to toe.

My cutman, Gus, goes to work on my battered face. First, he presses a towel against the cut above my left eye. He holds the towel in place with one hand as he shoves cotton swabs soaked with adrenaline chloride into my nostrils with the other. This is to stop my nosebleed, which restarted after the beating I took in Round 5.

Once the swabs are securely stuffed towards my brain, Gus presses an endswell—a small piece of smooth, freezing-cold metal—across the upper ridges of my cheekbones, trying to flush away the blood that is pooling there. This commonly-used method to reduce swelling may look soothing when you see it done on TV, but I can assure you it's not. The ridges of your cheekbones and eyebrows don't respond kindly to someone pressing a metal object as hard as possible against them.

After working the endswell, Gus frantically shifts his attention to closing the cut above my left eye. He spreads the wound wide apart with his fingers as he presses a cotton swab soaked in adrenaline chloride directly into the open wound—and yes, this is as painful as it sounds. Gus uses adrenaline chloride on almost everything. The solution is supposed to constrict the blood vessels and dam up the bleeding.

Now that he has stopped the bleeding above my left eye, Gus applies an ice pack to the welt just below my right eye.

You don't have to be a doctor to know that I'm in rough shape. The bleeding and the swelling can be slowed, but it can't be stopped if I keep taking punches. It's only a matter of time before one or both my eyes swell up to the point that the ref will have to call the fight. There's no way I'll last to the twelfth round in this condition.

With my headache worsening, my lungs burning, the metallic taste of blood running down my throat, and my face throbbing, I wish, for a moment, that this was all over.

I'm not in this guy's league. He's too strong. He's too fast. He's winning this fight. I wish I was lying down somewhere—anywhere—resting, relaxing, and recuperating for an hour, a day, a week. Every muscle and bone in my body wants nothing more than to…rest. *I gave it my best. I just don't have what it takes.*

"I know what you're feeling right now," Andre says, interrupting my thoughts. "You're sore, you're tired, and you're in pain. But all that is good."

I look at Andre for an explanation.

"It's good because it means you're alive," he says. "Patterson gave you the best he has and you're still here. You took his very best shots and this thing ain't over. He can't believe you're still standing. Nobody in this arena can. Nobody except the men in this corner.

"You got knocked down, but you got back up. That's all that matters. Who cares what happened in that last round? It's already in the past. It's over and done with. None of it matters. The pain is only temporary. It's what you do *next* that matters most. It's what you do *after* you get hit with adversity that determines your destiny.

"Mickey, this is your moment. This is your time. This is when you make the choice to be a champion or not."

As Andre says these words, I'm reminded that fear wants me to surrender. Fear is telling me I'm not good enough. Fear is telling me to quit. I have to counter the voice of fear.

This fight isn't over. My fate has not been decided. I control my destiny. What I do next is what matters most.

"Seconds out," the referee yells, telling the cornermen to exit the ring.

I stand up slowly. Gus rubs his concoction of Vaseline and more adrenaline chloride into my wounds. The purpose is two-fold: to restrict the blood vessels and to create a slick surface that punches will slip off of.

The bell rings and Round 6 begins.

As expected, Patterson comes rushing out of his corner. He assumes, correctly, that I'm still rubbery from the beating I took in the last round.

He gives me everything he has. Big, powerful punches. He's trying to end this fight and my only defense is to pull him in close and try to avoid getting caught with an uppercut as I do so. The pain worsens with each blow he lands, but he's also missing quite a few. Fatigue has made him less accurate.

I throw just enough punches to show the ref I'm defending myself.

Patterson backs off after his initial flurry. He's tired too.

Halfway through the round, Patterson throws a wild shot that grazes my chin. Unfortunately, I clumsily trip over my own feet trying to avoid the punch and I go down. I'm back up quickly, but the ref gives me a standing-eight count. I plead my case that it wasn't a knockdown because I tripped. The ref ignores my pleas.

Late in the round, I hit the canvas again. This time,

it's not a trip. Patterson lands a left to my right temple, making my ears ring again as I dizzily fall to the canvas.

I'm on one knee as the ref counts and, for a moment, I consider letting him finish the count. I hear the voice of fear whispering in my ear, *Stay down*.

But then, a thought rushes into my mind like a freight train blasting out of a dark tunnel. The thought says: ***Stay down and regret it forever or get up and make history right now***.

I pop up to a standing position and feel a surge of adrenaline. If I ever needed proof of just how powerful self-talk is, this is that proof. A quick change from negative to positive self-talk makes me feel like a new man.

Suddenly, I'm refreshed and reenergized. Not 100 percent, of course, but better than I've felt since the second round. I feel *alive*. I don't think about the pain and soreness. I'm sure it's still there, but I don't feel it because I don't think about it. Instead of envisioning myself as the hurting, bleeding man who just got knocked down for the third time in two rounds, I envision myself as a warrior who has just taken the best his opponent has and is still standing tall. I almost feel like raising my arms in victory right then and there.

Fear says to stay down. I say to stand tall.

"Bring it on," I yell to Patterson who is standing in the corner across from me as the ref finishes counting to eight.

The microphones near the ring pick up my challenge as I motion for Bruno to come my way. The crowd hears and sees this and they let out a rumble of excitement. That rumble builds to a thunderous ovation by the time the ref tells us to fight again.

Bruno Patterson gives just the slightest shake of his head. He can't believe I've gotten back up. He's got to be wondering what he has to do to keep me down.

We reengage at the center of the ring.

I will not go down again.

18

THE FEAR OF BEING "DUE" FOR A SETBACK

ONE WEEK EARLIER...

A week before the biggest fight of my life, I started to get this ominous feeling like something very bad was about to happen. Though I was nearing the end of the best training camp I'd ever had and I felt great physically, I couldn't shake the fear of impending doom.

After our training session for the day, I got cleaned up and asked Andre if I could talk with him.

"Of course," Andre said. "Have a seat."

I sat down on the edge of the ring canvas, which stood in the center of Andre's empty gym. The place had grown into a fully-operational boxing facility over the years and Andre now trained a few other fighters. We were the last ones here on this night.

In the eight years since Andre started training me, my relationship with him had grown into one of trust and respect. I could talk to him about anything and everything. We were like family. He no longer had to pry the negative thoughts and fears out of me. I was no longer embarrassed to tell him the truth about whatever feelings I was struggling with. I recognized when I needed his guidance.

"There's negative noise in my head," I said. "I can't quite put my finger on it."

"What kind of negative noise?" Andre asked.

"It's a feeling," I said. "A feeling that maybe this is as good as it gets and I'm about to fall hard."

"You don't think you can go toe-to-toe with Patterson?"

Andre had spent the last few months constantly reinforcing all the reasons why he thought I was going to be a matchup nightmare for the heavyweight champ. He had repeated those reasons so often that I believed them too.

"It's not that," I said. "I know I can go toe-to-toe with him. I *know* I've got what it takes to win."

"Then what is it?"

"Lately, I've been thinking about how lucky I am,"

I said. "I mean, next week I'm getting a shot at the heavyweight championship of the world. How crazy is that? It wasn't long ago that I was just a beat-up bartender wondering what I should do with my life. If you hadn't started training me when you did, who knows how different my life would be right now. At home, things are incredible. I have a wife who loves me and three healthy kids. We just bought a new house. What more could I ask for? Everything has been going so great lately. I feel so lucky, so blessed."

Andre chuckled. "How is any of this bad?"

"None of it's bad. And that's the problem. It's a little *too* good. I feel like I'm waiting for the other shoe to drop. I feel like things have been going so well for me lately that I'm heading for a fall. I'm just waiting for something to knock me back to reality—like I'm *due* for something bad to happen."

Andre's face turned serious as he listened to me. He nodded as if he knew exactly what I was feeling.

"That's another one of fear's favorite lies," he said. "The fear that you're due for something bad is a tough fear to shake. It's tough because it's rooted in past beliefs and experiences that are very strong emotionally. It's caused by something someone said to you repeatedly or something painful you experienced. Usually some of both. Is there anything in particular that happened in your past that might have planted the seeds for this fear to grow?"

I thought about it for a few seconds and said, "Yes, things I was told *and* things I experienced. I look back on my life and I see that every time things started going really well, it wasn't long before something bad happened."

"Like what?"

"Growing up, whenever things were going well in our house, my dad used to say, 'Enjoy it now because it's only a matter of time before things change.' I know he meant to enjoy life's good times, but whenever he said that, it always gave me a feeling of dread, of fear."

"As it would anybody," Andre said.

"And whenever something negative happened, he would shake his head and say, 'There's always something going wrong, isn't there?' My dad saw life as one long string of problems with a few good times sprinkled between them. He was a great man, but he liked to point out how the good times never lasted. And you know what? He was right. Whenever things were going great for us, it was only a matter of time before something really bad happened. Like my mom leaving our family right when I was getting to know her. Like my dad passing away right after celebrating his retirement. Look at my career in the ring. Every time I conquer one fear and take the next step, something comes along to stop me in my tracks and knock me back to reality."

"Life is always changing," Andre said. "There will always be new obstacles, but you can turn those obstacles into opportunities. You know this. We've talked about it a lot."

"I know," I said. "But this is different. This is a fear that says *because* things have been going so well, it's time for a reality check—like the good times aren't meant to last. It's such a strong fear. I know I sound like a pessimist, but I can't shake this feeling."

Andre gave another knowing nod. "It makes sense that this fear would show up right now. You're one week away from fighting for the very pinnacle of your profession. You know how special and rare it is to reach this level. You know how hard you've worked to get here. Most fighters never come close to reaching the heights you've reached. It's only natural that you'd have to face the fear of losing what you've worked so hard to achieve."

"That's exactly it. I feel like the guy who is a few feet away from the mountaintop and I'm just waiting to slip and fall all the way back down. Like once I start slipping, there will be no stopping my fall.

"How do I defeat this fear? It's weighing me down."

"You already know how to defeat it," Andre said.

I smiled. "Then I guess I could use a reminder."

"The fears you've dealt with over the years have all been different, but the solution to defeating each of them has always been the same: What you focus on is what you tend to create. If you want to change your attitude or your circumstances, simply change what you're focusing on. Shift your focus from fear of a negative outcome to faith in a positive one.

"Right now, the voice of fear is telling you that you're *due* for a setback. It's telling you to get ready for some bad times because things have been going too good, right?"

I nodded.

"And that fear has been reinforced by the things you heard and experienced growing up. That's what makes it a tough fear to defeat."

I nodded again, waiting for Andre's guidance on *how* to defeat this stubborn fear.

"You were conditioned from a young age to see life this way," Andre said. "You've been told to expect something bad after experiencing something good — maybe not in those exact terms, but the things you heard your father say created this belief in you. And, as you know, your beliefs and expectations tend to become your reality.

"The messages we receive when we're young lay the foundation for our beliefs and that's not always a good thing. Those negative beliefs we've embraced — often unknowingly — have to be rooted out.

"Your mom left you when you were young, right?"

"Yes," I said. "When I was nine."

"I dealt with something similar," Andre said. "I never knew my father and let's just say my mother would not have won any parenting awards. So, you and me both — from a very young age — were given the message that love is fleeting. It might be here one day and gone the next.

"You said your dad repeated the message that good times would never last and that something bad was always right around the corner. Well, that message obviously got into your head. Doesn't mean it was intentional or that your dad was a bad guy. As a cop, he surely saw a lot of rough stuff. You told me once how devastated he was when your mom left. Those pains probably made him jaded. From everything you've told me about your dad it sounds like he loved you, but some of his pessimistic views were clearly passed on to you.

"Here's the important thing to understand: the beliefs that were passed down to you don't have to be *accepted* by you. You can change your beliefs. You get to choose what you believe now and you can make sure those beliefs help you instead of hurt you.

"If you believe you're due for something bad to happen, you're going to find bad things to focus on. Do you think that helps you or hurts you?"

"Obviously, it's going to hurt me," I said. "But that *is* how life goes. The good times always seem like precursors to bad times."

"Believing that it's time for a setback becomes a self-fulfilling prophecy," Andre said. "If you think something bad is about to happen, you'll tend to create the circumstances for experiencing something bad. But the opposite is true as well.

"Whatever you go looking for, you'll tend to find. Go looking for bad things to happen and you'll find bad things to experience. Go looking for positive opportunities and you'll find them all around you.

"The beliefs you have and the things you choose to focus on create the environment you're most likely to experience.

"It all comes back to what you're choosing to focus on. **Your focus is your aim. Whatever you aim for, you're more likely to hit.** And even if you don't hit the bullseye, you still end up close to it.

"Let's look at how focus affects pain. As a fighter, you know all about pain. Whether it's the pain you feel in your legs during a hard run or the pain you feel after a world-class heavyweight slams his fist into your face, you get to choose what you focus on in those moments. Focus on the pain, and you'll feel more pain. Focus on how tired you are and how much everything hurts and you'll feel weaker. Your focus will amplify the pain.

"It's in those moments when you have to teach yourself not to focus on the pain, but to instead focus on the desired result or the positive consequences of pain. Focus on moving forward *despite* the pain and the pain lessens. Focus on fighting *through* the pain and the pain dissipates. Focus on the strength that comes *from* pain and the pain gives way to feelings of strength.

"What you focus on determines what you experience. Focus on the pain and you'll experience more pain. Focus on bad things and you'll notice all kinds of bad things around you. Focus on your weaknesses and you'll feel weaker. Focus on making excuses and you'll find excuses to make. Focus on your fears and they'll only get stronger.

"If someone believes they're *due* for a setback, where is their focus?"

"The setback," I said.

"Exactly. And if they're focused on experiencing a setback, they'll find one to experience. If you aim for a setback, you can't be surprised when you have one.

"See how this works? **The beliefs we hold onto drive everything. What you believe will determine what you focus on, which will determine what you experience.**

"The fear of being *due* for a fall isn't based on reality—it's based on a belief. You can choose to change your beliefs. Choose to believe you're due for something bad and you'll experience something bad. Choose to believe that good things are coming your way and you'll find the good in even the roughest situations. It's all up to what you choose to believe and focus on."

"This all sounds great," I said, "but you're making it sound like if I just believe everything is going to work out for me, it will. That's not how the world works."

"I suppose that depends on how you define *'working out for you,'*" Andre said. "If you think I'm saying you will never experience any setbacks in life as long as you don't go looking for them, you're misunderstanding me. You better believe I didn't go looking for a career-ending car wreck a week after winning a world title."

Andre's reminders of what he experienced were always well timed. He wasn't some head-in-the-clouds Pollyanna who had lived a charmed life. He had been through life's peaks and valleys and his beliefs were hard-won.

"Sometimes you will lose," Andre said. "In the ring and in any other area of life. That's true no matter what you're focusing on or how positive your expectations are. But I believe that even life's defeats can *'work out for you'* if you choose for them to.

"When you experience setbacks, you can choose what you focus on. You can focus on the pain of defeat. You can feel sorry for yourself and wallow in self-pity. Or, you can focus on what you learned from the setback. You can focus on all the ways that what you went through will make you better, stronger, and wiser.

"Whatever you go looking for, you will find. Fear wants you to go looking for the negatives. It's up to you to go looking for the positives.

"Your spiritual beliefs can also affect this fear of impending due. If you believe God is out to get you, just waiting for you to mess up, then you'll likely view the world as one big obstacle course where you're afraid of what might come next. If you believe God is out to help you, always by your side and giving you the strength and guidance to battle through whatever obstacle you may face, then you'll be excited about what might come next.

"I believe that no matter how bad a situation is, God will always bring a greater good out of it. It might not always be in this lifetime, but it *will* happen.

Ultimately, that's the greatest faith there is and it's the foundation for *everything* I believe. That faith has played out in my life. All the setbacks, defeats, and tragedies I've gone through have led me to something greater.

"With God's help, every tragedy can be turned into a triumph—I really believe that. No fear or defeat or setback is greater than the power of God. That belief forces me to focus on the positives that can come out of any negative situation. It keeps my focus on hope and strength and courage.

"Your inner beliefs determine your focus and what you focus on determines what you experience. **Don't hold onto any beliefs that empower fear. Choose only beliefs that empower *you*.**

"Mickey, I can't sit here and tell you that you'll never lose another fight if you only expect good things to happen. But I can tell you that expecting bad things to happen will almost certainly assure you of defeat."

Andre's words lingered in the quiet gym. He was right, of course. *Expecting* a defeat would all but guarantee a defeat.

"The good news," Andre continued, "is that it's not as hard as you may think to change the beliefs that have been imbedded within you. Just like conquering any other fear, it starts with recognizing the source of the fear. You've done that. Now you simply have to use your self-talk to combat those fears and to shift the focus from fear to faith.

"**When fear says, 'Bad things are headed your way.' Reverse it. Immediately say, '*Great* things are coming my way.'**

"**When fear says, 'Focus on the pain you feel.' You say, 'I am stronger than my pain.'**

"**When fear says, 'You're due for a setback.' You say, 'With God by my side, I can accomplish anything.'**

"Repeat these empowering words over and over. Fear wants you to think you have no control over your future or the beliefs you've accepted from your past, but fear is a liar. **You can conquer each and every fear you face by simply shifting the focus from fear to faith. Aim for what you want to have happen and not what you don't.**"

Over the next few days, as I prepared for my championship fight with Bruno Patterson, I made sure to start each morning in quiet prayer. I spoke openly with God, asking him for help, and then telling myself again and again, "Great things are coming my way!"

It sounded a little silly at first, like I was forcing myself to believe something I wasn't quite sure of. But the more I said it, the more I believed it. And the more I believed it, the more I *felt* it. I felt more confident, refreshed, and inspired to tackle the day ahead. I felt lighter — the pressure, fear, and worry lifting from my shoulders.

The confidence Andre had in God's power and goodness was contagious. In the days leading up to the fight, I made my self-talk more spiritual than usual. I repeated phrases such as, *I am blessed, I am strong, I am protected by God. God is taking care of me. With God by my side, I can accomplish anything.*

A couple hours before my fight with Patterson, alone in my locker room, I whispered a little prayer: "Thank you for this moment, thank you for being here with me. Whatever happens in the future, I trust you to guide me on the path I'm supposed to be on. I refuse to worry. I trust you with it all. Fill me with your love. Fill me with your power. Make me the best that I can be. Whatever happens happens. I trust you with the results. I trust you with everything."

That little prayer brought me a sense of peace I had

never before felt prior to a fight.

I promised myself right then that I wasn't ever going to let fear — any fear — have the upper hand on me. Though fear would continue to attack me throughout the night, I knew that with God's help I could defeat it.

I knew that though I may or may not win the fight against Bruno Patterson, I *would* win the fight against fear. That was all that mattered to me.

I promised myself to defeat fear and to leave the results in God's hands.

19

ROUND SEVEN

Patterson vs. McGavin
ROUND 7...

As I stand to begin Round 7, my vision is blurred in the lower half of my right eye and in the upper half of my left eye. Gus has done all he can to slow the swelling, but I know it's only going to get worse as this fight goes on. Time is not on my side.

As strange as it may sound, especially considering how beaten and bloodied I must look, I feel more confident right now than I have all night.

Something happened in Round 6 after I hit the canvas for the third time. I realized I have taken the worst punishment the champion can dish out...and it wasn't as bad as I had feared it would be.

Often times, the best way to defeat fear is to experience the very thing you fear. Everything I feared about facing Bruno Patterson — getting caught with an uppercut I never saw coming, getting knocked woozy and not being able to defend myself properly, exerting myself into exhaustion too early in the fight, getting cut, breaking my nose, getting pummeled by those powerful punches I saw him drop so many other top fighters with, getting knocked down and wondering if I could get back up — all those things I was afraid of before the fight have happened to me. And as I head into the seventh round, I realize none of it was that bad. It wasn't that good, either, but it wasn't as bad as I had made it out to be in my mind.

The fear of impending doom is almost always worse than the reality of experiencing whatever it is we fear. I have absorbed the champion's very best shots and the fear of what those shots would do to me was much worse than the reality of experiencing them.

"Attack and adapt," I hear Andre shout from behind me.

Once again, it's perfectly-timed advice from my friend and mentor. The things I have feared have happened and I will now do the only thing I know to do in the face of fear: *attack and adapt*.

Seconds before the bell rings to start Round 7, I say to myself: *I am strong. I am healthy. I am blessed. God is by my side. Nothing can stop me.*

The bell rings.

I surprise even myself how quickly I rush out of my corner.

Adrenaline fires through my body. I no longer feel the throbbing in my head. I no longer feel the burn of fatigue in my arms and legs. I no longer fear running out of time. I'm completely in the moment, focused only on the task at hand. Everything else fades away. All I'm thinking about is attacking and adapting, trusting my instincts.

What you focus on is what you experience. If I focus on the pain or what has happened thus far in the fight, that is what I will experience. If I focus on attacking and adapting in this very moment, that is what I will experience.

I choose to attack and adapt.

I use the peekaboo technique once again to get in close to Patterson. He flings a jab at my forehead. It lacks the pop it had earlier in the fight.

I slip inside and land a punishing right uppercut to his ribs just as he exhales. It lands with a loud thud.

It's the type of perfectly-timed shot that would drop most fighters. But Patterson isn't like most fighters. He's the heavyweight champion of the world. He grimaces and falls towards me, trying to protect the left side of his rib cage. He's so tall that I feel his gloves come down on the back of my head as he tries to pull me close enough that I can't punch anymore.

As he pulls me closer, I come up hard with a left uppercut that lands under his chin. It snaps his head back and I feel his arms loosen.

To the ribs I go again, machine-gun style: right-left-right-left-right-left, as fast as I can throw them.

Instincts tell me to adapt and I raise my gloves to protect my head just as the champ throws a right hook at me. I block his punch, take a step back, and fire two quick left jabs at his face.

He's in trouble. He reaches for me with outstretched arms. I slip underneath and land a right hook to his ribs. This time the loud thud is accompanied by a crunch as I feel his ribs give. I've just broken one or more of them. I'm sure of it.

The champion lowers himself as if he was on an elevator.

He takes a knee and holds his left side as the ref

sends me to my corner. I've scored a knockdown with a body shot.

Patterson winces with every breath he takes as the ref counts in front of him. Famous fights have ended on body shots. I hope this one will too.

As the referee hits seven, Patterson stands up and nods to the question he is asked. He's going to continue.

The fight resumes and I move in cautiously, just in case he's playing possum. I throw a couple left jabs at him, trying to get him to retaliate. I want to see how he throws his left. If it's weak and restricted, I'll know he's in a lot of pain...and in big trouble.

I throw two more cautious jabs as he holds his left elbow tight against his ribs and dodges me. He finally retaliates with a straight right that misses.

I instinctually counter with an overhand left that comes down hard on his right eyebrow. It's a shot that lands so squarely I don't even feel it—sort of like hitting a baseball with the sweet spot of the bat.

Almost immediately, I see blood. I've reopened the cut above his left eye. The crowd cheers as Patterson staggers backwards.

I throw a straight left that backs him into the

corner. He pulls his gloves to his face in a defensive position.

I throw a right hook that gets blocked by his forearm, but I follow that up with a quick left hook that connects with the side of his head. I see an opening in his guard and nail him with a straight right to the face, followed by a left uppercut that lands underneath his chin.

I'm not thinking. I'm not fearing. I'm completely in the moment, trusting my instincts.

Attack and adapt. Attack and adapt.

I *feel* the crowd's roar all around me.

I go downstairs and land a right hook to his ribs. Patterson lets out a grunt of agony.

As he drops his left shoulder to protect his rib cage with his elbow, I land the most devastating, perfectly-placed right hook I've ever landed.

It connects with the left side of his jaw. I see the bottom half of the champ's jaw swing to the right and it's lights out for Bruno Patterson.

As he falls to the canvas, his mouthpiece spills out.

He lands first on his knees, then falls forward and hits the canvas face-first.

He's not out cold, but I can tell he doesn't know

where he is as he rolls to his side.

As the referee counts, Patterson reaches for a rope to pull himself up, but he loses his balance and his massive arm awkwardly slips between the bottom two ropes.

He pulls his arm away from the ropes and then gets on his hands and knees. He holds that position, tries to catch his breath, and then looks up towards me. He shakes his head slightly and I can see he's done. He's not trying to get up anymore.

The referee reaches the count of ten and the bell rings multiple times as the crowd thunders.

The fight is over.

I have won one of the most dramatic and action-packed heavyweight championship bouts ever fought.

Andre is the first person into the ring and he's followed by a swarm of reporters, cornermen, and boxing officials.

I raise my arms in victory and for the first time since Round 7 began, I realize how tired they are.

My adrenaline gives way to exuberance. Make that, *relief*. I really don't know if I'm more excited to be the heavyweight champion of the world or relieved to have the toughest fight of my career over with.

I wrap my arms around Andre for a tight hug. "Thank you," I say. "Thank you for everything."

"You did it," Andre says. "I'm proud of you!"

As he says those words, I think of my dad. I can feel him saying the same thing.

I look up to the heavens.

"Thank you," I say quietly. "Thank you."

★★★ 20 ★★★
POSTFIGHT

Patterson vs. McGavin

HOURS AFTER THE FIGHT…

I have celebrated the victory with Andre, my family, and my cornermen. I've been checked over and stitched up by the on-site doctors. I have answered all the post-fight questions from reporters.

Finally, I make it back to my hotel room and after a hot shower I fall, cautiously, into my bed. Rachel is beside me, already asleep.

Since the fight ended, I've been rushed from one thing to the next. Now, I am alone with my thoughts. I want to take in this surreal moment before I fall asleep.

I am the heavyweight champion of the world.

It doesn't feel real. I'm half-expecting to wake up from a dream.

Lying on my back for the first time since being knocked to the ring canvas earlier this evening, I slowly untense my tired and aching muscles. I feel my body sink into the bed. I don't think I've ever been more grateful for a place to rest.

I close my eyes and think with amazement about how all this happened.

Ten years ago, I left college to pursue my dream of becoming a professional boxer. Eight years ago, I was fired by my manager, before meeting the man who would change my life. Less than two years ago, I thought it was time to hang up my gloves and retire.

Tonight, I am the heavyweight champion of the world.

I reflect on how I got here. How I went from being a timid, indecisive fighter loaded with fear and uncertainty to becoming the fearless fighter who just knocked out the unbeatable Bruno Patterson.

How did this happen? How?

I smile. My face hurts when I smile, but I smile anyway. I can't believe it. My wildest dream has come true.

My life changed when Andre Holiday started teaching me how to defeat my fears. Fear held me back from being the man I was capable of becoming. When I stopped listening to the voice of fear, I started becoming the man I was born to be. Once I learned to defeat fear, everything changed.

Andre taught me that everything in life is a choice. Especially how we deal with fear. **We get to choose whether or not we're going to let fear defeat us. It's our choice, no one else's.**

Whenever I see someone wallowing in self-pity or engaging in self-destructive behavior, I now know that I'm seeing someone giving in to their fears. They are letting fear hold them back. They are letting fear defeat them.

I was once that person. I promise myself to never again be that person.

No matter what happens from this moment on, in the ring or out, I know that I can move forward in faith — the faith and confidence that I am more powerful than the fear that tries to stop me. Fear will never again get the best of me.

When fear throws its best punches at me, I will counter them with power shots of my own.

When fear says, "You don't belong here, nobody thinks you have what it takes." I will say, "**I am** listening to my heart and living my God-given purpose. I have the power to succeed."

When fear says, "Seek safety by keeping everything the same." I will say, "**I seek victory by changing and growing.**"

When fear says, "Don't make a decision until you're certain you can't be wrong." I will say, "**There is no such certainty, I move forward by attacking, adapting, and learning as I go.**"

When fear says, "It's time to move on, it's time to quit, there's an easier way than this." I will say, "**I am** *all in.* **I am moving forward with grit and perseverance. Success does not require shortcuts; success requires total commitment.**"

When fear says, "You're not good enough. You don't deserve success." I will say, "**I have the power to determine what I deserve. The bigger I dream and the harder I work, the higher I will climb.**"

When fear says, "Because you failed, you will fail again. Stay down and quit!" I will say, "**Because I failed, I am stronger and wiser than ever before. Get up and keep fighting!**"

When fear says, "You're due for a setback, bad things are headed your way." I will say, "**I am** blessed, I am strong, I am protected by God. Great things are coming my way."

Fear is the ultimate opponent. Just like the opponents I face in the ring, the only way to defeat fear is to fight back. I will never again sit back and passively accept fear's favorite lies. I will fight back with positive, faith-filled self-talk. I will not let fear defeat me. Not in the ring and not in any other area of my life.

As long as I do not allow fear to defeat me, I can live with whatever results I get.

Andre once told me, "**There are two types of people in this world: Those who believe success is a choice and those who make excuses for why they're not successful.**"

Everyone is walking into the unknown. Nobody knows what tomorrow will bring. You can choose to walk forward in faith or fear. Champions choose faith. Champions choose to be fearless. Why? Because victory favors the fearless.

Everything is a choice. I choose to be fearless.

About the Author

DARRIN DONNELLY is a writer and entrepreneur. He and his products have been featured in publications such as *The Wall Street Journal*, *Sports Illustrated*, *Fast Company Magazine*, and newspapers, websites, and radio outlets all over the world. He lives in Kansas City with his wife and three children.

Donnelly can be reached at *SportsForTheSoul.com* or on Twitter: @DarrinDonnelly.

Sports for the Soul

Stories of Faith, Family, Courage, and Character.

This book is part of the *Sports for the Soul* series. For updates on this book, a sneak peek at future books, and a free newsletter that delivers advice and inspiration from top coaches, athletes, and sports psychologists, join us at: **SportsForTheSoul.com**.

The *Sports for the Soul* newsletter will help you:
- Find your calling and follow your passion
- Harness the power of positive thinking
- Build your self-confidence
- Attack every day with joy and enthusiasm
- Develop mental toughness
- Increase your energy and stay motivated
- Explore the spiritual side of success
- Be a positive leader for your family and your team
- Become the best version of yourself
- And much more…

Join us at: **SportsForTheSoul.com**.

Collect the previous books in the Sports for the Soul series...

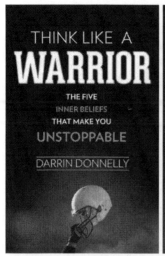

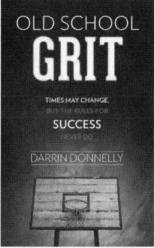

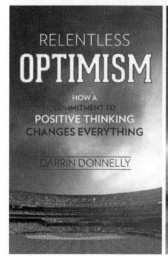

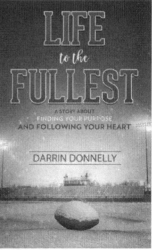

Visit SportsForTheSoul.com

Book No. 1 in the *Sports for the Soul* series…

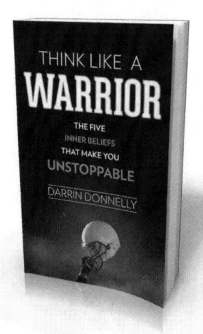

Think Like a Warrior
by Darrin Donnelly

In this bestselling inspirational fable, a college football coach at the end of his rope receives mysterious visits from five of history's greatest coaches: **John Wooden, Buck O'Neil, Herb Brooks, Bear Bryant, and Vince Lombardi**. Together, these legendary leaders teach him the five inner beliefs shared by the world's most successful people. The "warrior mindset" he develops changes his life forever — and it will change yours as well.

Book No. 2 in the *Sports for the Soul* series...

Old School Grit

by Darrin Donnelly

An old-school college basketball coach who thinks like John Wooden and talks like Mike Ditka enters the final NCAA tournament of his legendary career and uses his last days as a coach to write letters to the next generation revealing his rules for a happy and successful life: the 15 rules of grit. Consider this book an instruction manual for getting back to the values that truly lead to success and developing the type of old school grit that will get you through anything.

Book No. 3 in the *Sports for the Soul* series…

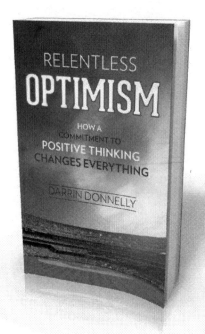

Relentless Optimism
by Darrin Donnelly

A minor-league baseball player realizes his lifelong dream of making it to the majors is finally coming to an end. That is, until he meets an unconventional manager who teaches him that if he wants to change his outcomes in life, he must first change his attitude. This book will show you just how powerful a positive attitude can be and it will teach you how to use positive thinking to make your biggest dreams come true.